U.S. Relations with
the World Bank
1945–1992

Brookings Occasional Papers

U.S. Relations with the World Bank 1945–1992

CATHERINE GWIN

THE BROOKINGS INSTITUTION
Washington, D.C.

7-26-99

Brookings Occasional Papers

THE BROOKINGS INSTITUTION is a private nonprofit organization devoted to research, education, and publication on important issues of domestic and foreign policy. Its principal purpose is to bring knowledge to bear on the major policy problems facing the American people.

On occasion Brookings authors produce research papers that warrant immediate circulation as contributions to the public debate on current issues of national importance. Because of the circumstances of their production, these Occasional Papers are not subjected to all of the formal review procedures established for the Institution's research publications, and they may be revised at a later date. As in all Brookings publications, the judgments, conclusions, and recommendations presented in the papers are solely those of the authors and should not be attributed to the trustees, officers, or other staff members of the Institution.

Copyright © 1994 by
THE BROOKINGS INSTITUTION
1775 Massachusetts Avenue, N.W., Washington, D.C.

ISBN 0-8157-3349-6

Library of Congress Catalog Number 94-072003

9 8 7 6 5 4 3 2 1

Acknowledgments

This paper was prepared as one of a series of essays commissioned in support of a project on the history of the World Bank. It will be included along with the other essays in a forthcoming volume. The Brookings Institution gratefully acknowledges financial support for the overall project provided by the following:

The Ford Foundation
The John D. & Catherine T.
  MacArthur Foundation
Japan Center for International
  Finance
Nikko Securities Company, Ltd.
Nomura Securities Company, Ltd.
Daiwa Securities Company, Ltd.
Haldor Topsøe A/S (Denmark)
Landsvirkjun, The National
  Power Company (Iceland)
A/S Veidekke (Norway)
Statkraft SF (Norway)
The World Bank

Deutsche Bank AG
The Japan Foundation
The Life Insurance Association
  of Japan
The Federation of Bankers
  Association of Japan
Yamaichi Securities Company, Ltd.
F. L. Smidth Company & Co. A/S
  (Denmark)
Reykjavik Hot Water System
  (Iceland)
Swedish Bankers Association
Central Bank of Norway
Asea Brown Boveri AS

Author's Acknowledgements

I wish to give special thanks to Brian Crowe, John Lewis, Eugene Rotberg, Jonathan Sandford, Richard Webb, Joe Wood, and especially Devash Kapur for advice and review of drafts of this paper. I also wish to thank James Schneider for editing the paper, Mary Ann Noyer for verifying its factual accuracy, and Susan Woollen for setting it in type.

THROUGHOUT THE HISTORY of the International Bank for Reconstruction and Development (the World Bank), the United States has been the largest shareholder and most influential member country. U.S. support for, pressures on, and criticisms of the Bank have been central to its growth and the evolution of its policies, programs, and practices. The United States, in turn, has benefited substantially in both foreign policy and economic terms from the Bank's promotion of development. The benefits have been especially significant during the past two decades as U.S. bilateral development aid has dwindled.

Underlying this half century of U.S.–World Bank relations has been a fundamental ambivalence on the part of the United States toward both development assistance and multilateral cooperation. On the one hand U.S. support for foreign aid generally and the Bank specifically has been guided by the view that promoting economic growth and development in other parts of the world is in the national interest and that multilateral cooperation is a particularly effective way of both leveraging and allocating resources for development. U.S. policy toward the Bank, led by the Treasury Department, has consistently emphasized these points. On the other hand the United States has viewed all multilateral organizations, including the World Bank, as instruments of foreign policy to be used in support of specific U.S. aims and objectives. Thus while it has supported the Bank for its capacity as a multilateral institution to leverage funds and influence borrowing countries' economic development policies, the United States has been uneasy with both the autonomy on which the Bank's development role depends and the power sharing that accompanies burden sharing. And the United States is often impatient with the processes of consensus building on which multilateral cooperation rests.

This ambivalence, a preoccupation with containing communism, and the change in the relative U.S. power in the world explain much of the evolution in U.S. relations with the World Bank over the past fifty years. In addition, the U.S. Congress, unlike the legislators in other Bank

1

member countries, has been a major influence on policy. Within the context of changing foreign policy concerns, congressional involvement has significantly affected the tenor and style of U.S. participation in the Bank. Having led in the establishment, early financial growth, and encouragement of the Bank's program expansion, the United States was by the 1970s at odds within itself over issues of foreign policy and foreign aid and frequently at odds with the Bank over its rate of growth and specific aspects of its operations. The development constituency, which had never been strong, was shattered, with groups on both the Left and the Right increasingly vocal in their criticisms of the Bank. After a supportive Carter administration was unable to knit the constituency together anew, the first Reagan administration added, for the first time, an executive branch voice to the chorus of multilateral aid opponents. The debt crisis in the south and the collapse of communism in eastern Europe led to renewed U.S. interest in the Bank. Simultaneously, pressure from nongovernmental organizations caused the U.S. government to push for increased Bank attention to the environment. However, renewed attention to the Bank was accompanied through the 1980s and into the early 1990s by both a continuing decrease in the U.S. share of Bank funding and a unilateral (at times dogmatic) assertiveness on matters of Bank policy, a combination that antagonized other member countries.

U.S. Leadership in Launching the Bank

Well before the end of World War II the United States began to plan for the economic recovery that would follow the peace. The aim of the postwar planning was to design a system of international economic cooperation that would avoid a repetition of the beggar-thy-neighbor trade and currency practices of the interwar period and instead encourage economic stability, full employment, and rising levels of income through the growth of international trade and investment.

Both the International Monetary Fund (IMF) and the International Bank for Reconstruction and Development were the results of that planning effort. In contrast to the Fund, which was the outcome of intense negotiation between the United States and Britain, the Bank was largely an American creation.[1] The United States proposed its basic design and led the effort to get it off the ground. From 1945 through 1960 it provided much of the Bank's top management and staff, the active support needed for its early institutional growth and policy expansion, and, through the U.S. market, most of the capital for lending. The result was a strong and enduring American imprint on all aspects of the Bank, including its structure, general policy direction, and forms of lending. Although this early history has been much written about, a number of points are worth repeating because they indicate the underlying U.S. perspective on the Bank and have proved central to the Bank's operations.

The White Plan

Work on a plan for an international bank began within the U.S. government in 1941.[2] In the interwar period many countries that had borrowed heavily from private banks defaulted on their commercial obligations. The international bank, designed largely by Harry Dexter White, adviser to the U.S. Treasury, was meant to overcome that legacy by facilitating an international flow of private investment and by encouraging countries to use financing effectively. Convinced that private investors could not be relied on to provide the net flow of dollars that would be needed for postwar reconstruction and development, he conceived of the Bank as an institution that would guarantee foreign securities and when necessary lend directly to governments. "The primary aim of such an agency should be to encourage private capital to go abroad for productive investment by sharing the risks of private investors in large ventures."[3] The initial capital of the Bank was set at $10 billion, an amount thought adequate for this catalytic task.[4] Participation by other countries in the Bank's design was minimal. John Maynard Keynes is reputed to have said that the United States got it wrong, that the International Monetary Fund should have been a bank and the Bank a fund. He also observed that the draft Bank document, "stripped, as it had long since been, of all exciting features," was "an uninspiring one . . . dressed, with an eye to Congress, to look as orthodox as possible."[5] Nevertheless, most countries, including the United Kingdom, refrained from taking much initiative on the plan because they did not expect to be in a position after the war to make significant contributions.

The Bank that emerged from the planning effort "was not created neutral."[6] U.S. views regarding how the world economy should be organized, how resources should be allocated, and how investment decisions should be reached were enshrined in the Charter and the operational policies of the Bank. This included the decision that the Bank should not lend directly to private enterprises. Two other early decisions reflected strong U.S. preferences for close oversight of the Bank by national representatives: the choice of a permanent site for the headquarters of the Bank and the definition of the role of the executive directors.[7] Britain, joined by many other countries, urged that the Bank be located outside the United States, but once it became clear that the United States would not agree, they sought at least to locate the headquarters in New York rather than Washington. As Keynes said, this was necessary to keep the institutions "clear of 'the politics of Congress and the nationalistic whispering gallery of the Embassies and Legations.'"[8] But the United States was strongly committed to Washington. The aim of Treasury Secretary Henry Morgenthau in the postwar planning effort was "to move the financial center of the world from London and Wall Street to the United States Treasury, and to create a new concept among nations in international finance." The new institutions were to be "instrumentalities of sovereign governments and not of private financial interests."[9]

This same perspective shaped the U.S. position on the role of the Bank's directors. In debating the duties of the executive directors, Britain (supported by some Commonwealth and European countries) sought again to minimize the influence of national governments. It argued that the directors should be officials resident in their home countries who would visit the Bank at regular intervals to deal with matters of high policy and leave the day-to-day affairs of the organization to management and staff. In contrast, the United States, which was committing the most money, insisted that the directors serve full time and exercise more initiative and control over operations and policy. Keynes made a strong and bitter speech on this matter and finally refused to vote for the U.S. formula. But the U.S. view prevailed.

The arrangement, and especially the function of the first U.S. executive director, Emilio Collado, led to a power struggle between the first few Bank presidents and the board—notwithstanding that the presidents were American citizens closely tied to the U.S. government. According to Davidson Sommers, an early member of the Bank's staff, "in the beginning [there] was the Board. . . . They, not too harmoniously but very effectively, assumed the initiative in organizing and running the affairs of the Bank. . . . [But] what was really important was the very predominant position of the American Director on the Board and the role that he played." Although no loans were actually made until 1947, it was "the normal thing for an applicant for a loan to stop on his way to the Bank and get the support of the U.S. Director."[10] Interestingly, Collado was an appointee from the State Department, not, as later became the rule, from Treasury.

The situation produced a great deal of tension and led to the early resignation of the Bank's first president, Eugene Meyer, out of frustration with his position vis-à-vis the U.S. director.

> Partly because of disputes between member nations, most particularly the United States and Britain, and partly because of distrust on Wall Street, he had not been able to sell a single bond or issue any development loans. He had also found himself embroiled in a debilitating conflict with his own board of executive directors, in particular the U.S. executive director. . . . "Pete" Collado had spent his entire professional life in the Roosevelt administration, working with such liberal personalities as Harry Dexter White at the Treasury Department and Alger Hiss in the State Department. Meyer consequently considered him a brash young New Dealer, and they didn't get along. Collado and the executive directors from other nations believed Meyer should run the Bank according to policy voted upon by the board. They were eager to issue as many loans as possible, and quickly. When Meyer refused one day to approve an early loan to Chile, Collado pounded the table, demanding that the loan be approved. Meyer calmly refused, saying the Bank was not a relief agency. But such constant disputes with Collado took their toll on the seventy-one-year-old Meyer, and in December 1946 he resigned. He told his secretary, "I could stay and fight these bastards, and probably win in the end, but I'm too old for that."[11]

In consultation with other members of the executive board, the United States approached several prominent bankers to succeed Meyer, including Graham F. Towers, governor of the Bank of Canada. But Towers declined, saying that a U.S. citizen had to lead the Bank if its credibility on Wall Street was to be established. The United States then turned to John J. McCloy, a Wall Street lawyer. "Some of McCloy's Wall Street colleagues saw in his possible appointment an opportunity to take control of the World Bank away from the New Deal crowd represented by 'Morgenthau and those clucks.'"[12] But despite Wall Street's enthusiasm, McCloy initially turned down the offer on the grounds that the Bank's Articles of

Agreement placed a preponderance of power in the hands of the directors. This would make the intervention of politics into lending decisions inevitable and, as a result, make it difficult to sell Bank loans.

McCloy changed his decision only after the United States and the rest of the board accepted conditions defining his role and after he was satisfied that the only potential buyers of Bank bonds, the New York commercial banks and insurance companies, were likely to cooperate. His conditions were that first, the United States would not interfere in loan negotiations; in particular, loan applicants would be directed to the Bank's management and not given a prior indication of the U.S. position. Second, the Bank president would have a free hand in administrative matters, including the hiring and firing of staff. Third, McCloy would nominate the U.S. executive director. Although the conditions were rejected by U.S. government officials, President Truman overruled his advisers and told McCloy that the United States would accept them.[13] Collado was subsequently replaced by Eugene Black who, on McCloy's insistence, simultaneously took charge of the Bank's bond operations.[14]

In the summer of 1949 McCloy resigned to assume the position of high commissioner in Germany and urged that Black be appointed to succeed him. Given his assertive style, McCloy's tenure had created substantial tensions with the Board, especially with the non-American members, who objected to the American "monopoly" in the Bank. Although Black did much to relieve the tensions, he also continued the practice of nominating the U.S. director and continued to rely heavily on and work closely with both the U.S. government and its director.

The decisions on the Bank's location and the role of its directors, which were to have profound effects on its operations, facilitating daily interaction between the Bank and the U.S. government and frequent political intrusion into Bank decisionmaking by all member governments, reflected U.S. ambivalence toward multilateral cooperation. But these features also contributed to broad-based and strong support for the Bank in Congress and with the public.

Congressional Approval

When the legislation authorizing U.S. participation in the Bank and the IMF was submitted to Congress, the House voted 345–18 in favor and the Senate 61–16.[15] The administration based its advocacy for U.S. membership on the importance of the two institutions ensuring the stability of the postwar economy. Treasury Secretary Morgenthau told Congress that the Bretton Woods plan was "the first practical test of our willingness to cooperate in the work of world reconstruction [and] one very important step towards the orderly, expanding foreign trade on which our agriculture and industry depends." Assistant Secretary of State Dean Acheson told Congress that the proposal represented a chance to avoid the disaster of international warfare "by acting in common with the other nations of the world to put aside the implements of economic warfare and make possible an expansion of production and consumption and trade." Assistant Treasury Secretary Harry Dexter White emphasized further that the plan was necessary for international economic peace, economic prosperity, and the revitalization of markets for U.S. goods.[16]

In its deliberations Congress made two changes in the legislation submitted by the administration. The first called for the creation of a National Advisory Committee on International Monetary and Financial Problems. This was to be a cabinet-level committee chaired by the secretary of the Treasury and composed of heads of other departments. It was "to coordinate the policies and operations of the representatives of the United States."[17] In a second change, Congress required that the executive branch obtain prior authorization on major decisions regarding U.S. participation in the Fund and Bank.

A minority report issued by a small group of conservative senators denounced the Bretton Woods Act for starting the United States "on a permanent policy of foreign lending and investment by Americans in huge sums, sponsored and to a large extent guaranteed by the Federal Government."[18] For the most part, however, the Bretton Woods initiative received strong support from a wide range of national groups and from a bipartisan majority of Congress and swiftly "moved through the Congress on soaring hopes for a better world."[19]

The "Dollar Bank"

With that broad-based endorsement the U.S. government undertook actively to help sell the World Bank to the U.S. financial market.[20] This task dominated the administrations of the first three Bank presidents and largely determined the shape of Bank lending in its first decade.

The original U.S. capital subscription was $3,175 million or 34.9 percent of the $9,100 million total.[21] Its overall contribution to the financial start-up of the Bank was far greater, however. Of the Bank's total initial capitalization of $10 billion, 20 percent was to be paid in and 80 percent held in reserve by member countries. Of the 20 percent paid in, 10 percent was to be in gold or dollars and 90 percent in the currency of each member country. During the Bank's first ten years, except for Canada's payment of part of its subscription in U.S. dollars and a few small payments from other countries, the U.S. subscription was the only fully usable subscription. Not until other currencies became convertible and economies recovered did this situation change. Also during the initial ten years, 85 percent of World Bank bonds were denominated in U.S. dollars and most were sold in the U.S. market. For related reasons, the only portion of the 80 percent "callable" reserves considered a significant guarantee to investors was the U.S. share. This became evident in 1958 when the spread between the volume of outstanding debt and the amount of the U.S. guarantee narrowed to only about $700 million, and the U.S. bond market rating services sounded the alarm. In effect, until well into the 1960s, Bank borrowing was limited by the amount of the U.S. share of the guarantee reserve.

It had been expected that the Bank would operate by guaranteeing securities issued by others rather than by issuing bonds of its own. But in 1946 U.S. efforts to enlist the interest of banking and insurance groups made clear that large investors would prefer to hold Bank securities rather than the securities of foreign governments backed by guarantees from the Bank.[22] Two obstacles confronted early efforts to sell Bank securities, however. The Bank did not fit under existing state banking laws and regulations, and, as a legacy of the interwar period, investment in foreign securities was considered risky. The U.S. government actively confronted both obstacles. The U.S. executive director took the lead in campaigning for the necessary changes in state legislation, and other officials helped the Bank's president to inform the investment community about the Bank's nature and policies.[23] These efforts quickly paid off: by the mid-1950s, Bank issues had achieved an AAA rating in the U.S. market and had begun to attract interest from non-American investors. In addition, until the early 1960s the Treasury Department gave its required consent for the issue of dollar-denominated Bank securities as a matter of course.

In this early period, Bank lending policies were conditioned by the necessity of finding U.S. investors who were willing to buy the Bank's securities and accept its guarantee. The management's view that the Bank's credit standing depended on the character of its loans led to an early emphasis on financing capital infrastructure and little lending in the social sectors.[24] By the start of the 1960s, however, the lending policy was less constrained by the attitudes of U.S. investors, in part because investor confidence had by then been established by the cautious policies Bank management had pursued and in part because investors had a better understanding of the Bank's role in promoting economic growth and development. Meanwhile, the relative importance of the U.S. market as a source of Bank borrowing began to decline (even though in absolute terms the volume of sales of dollar securities continued to increase). From 1956 to 1962–63 the Bank not only saw the release of capital subscriptions from its major European contributors but also succeeded in tapping non-U.S. markets for more of its capital. In the mid-1960s, confronted with a balance of payments deficit, the U.S. Treasury for the first time briefly denied the Bank access to its capital market and most Bank funds had to be raised elsewhere. And by the late 1960s more than half the Bank's dollar borrowings were being bought by investors outside the United States.

At the end of the decade, incoming Bank President Robert McNamara, with U.S. encouragement, accelerated this trend in portfolio diversification. His aim was not only to escape the effects of U.S. macroeconomic policy on the Bank, but also to lay the foundation for a sharp rise in Bank borrowing sufficient to enable lending to double. The change in medium- and long-term borrowing is shown in table 1. With U.S. support having helped build a strong financial position, portfolio diversification was not a difficult task. But it was one of a number of early signals of changing U.S. relations with the Bank that followed the shift in the Bank's focus from postwar reconstruction to development and accompanied the gradual decline of U.S. predominance in the postwar world economy.

The Shift to Development

As it quickly became clear that needed postwar reconstruction would exceed the resources of the newly created World Bank, the United States initiated the Marshall Plan as a separate recovery program for Europe and helped the Bank turn its attention to its second objective, development. But with the Bank's shift to the problems of development, the support of the United States, which remained dominant, became more hesitant and more conditional than at the outset.

Table 1. World Bank Medium- and Long-Term Borrowings, by Country before Swaps and by Currency after Swaps, Fiscal Years 1971–91
Millions of U.S. dollars

	Country					Currency				
Year	France	Germany	Japan	United Kingdom	United States	French franc	German mark	Japanese yen[a]	U.K. pound	U.S. dollar
1971	3	296	229	0	400	0	296	219	0	775
1972	6	347	160	37	425	31	342	150	24	796
1973	5	387	614	25	0	0	371	606	0	440
1974	6	235	471	25	0	0	220	461	0	659
1975	5	526	129	5	500	0	512	121	0	2,515
1976	4	707	197	19	1,275	0	859	0	0	2,152
1977	4	1,412	20	13	1,250	0	1,394	7	0	2,181
1978	4	1,149	582	5	1,360	0	1,120	646	0	2,099
1979	6	1,033	1,191	63	0	0	1,016	1,176	0	666
1980	9	1,993	1,288	5	0	0	2,256	1,266	0	694
1981	12	1,326	971	237	0	0	1,522	1,091	216	1,611
1982	7	738	1,337	266	1,687	0	1,229	1,341	311	2,602
1983	7	1,134	1,267	8	2,041	0	1,519	1,326	321	2,036
1984	11	1,382	1,579	152	0	0	1,838	1,700	421	1,170
1985	8	1,500	1,890	146	911	0	1,927	2,199	323	1,870
1986	147	1,609	2,036	136	429	-6	2,080	1,946	131	1,478
1987	9	1,392	1,461	20	1,107	0	1,897	3,383	73	1,757
1988	192	404	4,711	5	2,404	177	1,524	5,431	596	2,849
1989	7	716	3,782	64	822	161	657	3,754	8	5,522
1990	14	1,709	2,274	0	449	178	3,372	2,618	0	5,232
1991	5	919	611	0	114	11	3,094	1,262	4	4,519

Source: World Bank annual reports.

a. Numbers in the data for Japan are elevated because of refinancing. Refinancing data for 1987–89 are available and must be subtracted from totals.

In 1947 Britain withdrew its troops from the civil war raging in Greece, an act that precipitated the Truman Doctrine. The world, Truman said, faced a stark choice between two ways of life: communism and democracy. In this unfolding context, U.S. policy toward World Bank lending took on new political ramifications. In the face of mounting Communist party pressures in Europe, John McCloy and other leading Americans insisted that European recovery required assistance so massive that it surpassed the Bank's capacity. The effort, they argued, would have to be financed by the American taxpayer through a bilateral economic recovery program, first publicly proposed by Secretary of State George

Marshall. While still president of the Bank, McCloy lobbied vigorously for what came to be known as the Marshall Plan, explaining that Bank lending was constrained by the need to sell its securities in the financial markets. He also resisted U.S. pressure to have the Bank fund food aid to Western Europe as a temporary measure until Marshall Plan aid arrived. The Bank, McCloy insisted, was no substitute, even in the interim, for massive bilateral, politically motivated aid.[25]

Following the launching of the Marshall Plan, McCloy turned the Bank's attention to the less developed countries, beginning with Latin America. However, as constituted the Bank was ill-prepared to assume a major role in development financing. Its financial resources were too small, and many of the world's poorest countries could not afford its near-market rates. Moreover, the Articles of Agreement prohibited lending directly to private enterprises. As a result of these and other constraints, Bank lending to developing countries increased only slowly. Pressure to resolve these problems led ultimately to the establishment of the Bank's two affiliates, the International Finance Corporation (IFC) in 1956 and the International Development Association (IDA) in 1960, but only after the United States dropped its opposition and agreed to support them. In both cases the U.S. endorsement was given grudgingly, as much in response to foreign policy considerations as to the challenges of development.

An IFC and an IDA linked to the World Bank were proposed in 1951 by a U.S. advisory group appointed by President Truman to recommend ways to achieve the objectives of the Point Four Program. Point Four in Truman's 1949 inaugural address had called for a new program to make the benefits of scientific advances and industrial progress available to underdeveloped areas. A leading purpose of the new program was to strengthen key countries in the third world, particularly those surrounding the emerging Soviet bloc, and to dissuade others from aligning with the Soviets. Emphasizing the link between U.S. security interests and economic development in the third world, the program marked a historic turn in U.S. relations with developing countries and the beginnings of substantial U.S. foreign aid commitments to non-European countries.

In making its recommendations, the advisory group emphasized the need for some form of international machinery "for employing the techniques which lay between pure loans and pure grants," and it urged that the United States not undertake the development assistance task on its own.[26] It proposed that the United States take the lead in establishing both an IFC and an IDA affiliated with the World Bank, the IFC to mobilize capital for direct lending to the private sector and the IDA to provide concessional loans to poor countries using funds contributed by governments. These recommendations elicited no immediate U.S. government response, however. The United States was at war in Korea, it was faced with a growing budget deficit, and it was not yet convinced that more was needed to stimulate development, despite mounting pressure from developing countries within the United Nations for larger amounts of development funds on softer terms.

Frustrated by their inability to afford World Bank loans at market rates and emboldened by the perceived largesse of the Marshall Plan, developing countries had begun arguing in the late 1940s and early 1950s for the establishment of a new UN development agency that would provide technical and financial assistance on concessional terms and that would operate under the UN rule of one country, one vote, rather than under the Bank and its system of weighted voting. The United States strongly opposed a series of such proposals, but in 1954 abruptly endorsed the idea of the IFC as a political concession.[27] Concerned with the escalating cold war and Soviet attempts to exploit the UN debate between developed and developing countries, the United States determined that some response was necessary. "The State Department urged that the United States must make at least a gesture; and, this having been decided in principle, the government looked around for the cheapest thing to do, and the cheapest thing to do was the IFC."[28] In the request to Congress for support, President Eisenhower emphasized the IFC's potential contribution to "prosperity, expanded trade, and 'the peace and solidarity of the free world.'"[29] The proposal passed in both the House and Senate with little debate and a wide margin of support.[30]

Establishment of the IFC did not, however, stem developing countries' demands for a new concessional aid agency, to which the United States remained opposed until Congress broke the stalemate. In 1958 the Senate endorsed a proposal of one of its members, Mike Monroney of Oklahoma, for an international development agency linked to the World Bank that would use surplus unconvertible currency held by rich nations to fund projects in developing countries. As presented, Monroney's plan would have been costless but largely ineffectual. However, the favorable domestic response the Senator's proposal received, combined with the growing pressure from developing countries for a Special UN Fund for Economic Development (SUNFED), finally convinced the United States, in consultation with the World Bank's president, to present the executive board with a plan for the International Development Association. The plan for what became the Bank's concessional or soft loan window was accepted and submitted to governments for approval in January 1960.

The fact that many developing countries were quickly reaching the limits of their creditworthiness in Bank terms contributed to the U.S. decision to launch IDA. This problem had already led to the start-up in 1958 of the U.S. Development Loan Fund, a large bilateral concessional capital transfer operation, and to collaboration between Bank President Eugene Black and the Undersecretary of State Douglas Dillon on the launching of the India aid consortium, the first effort of its kind. In presenting the IDA proposal to Congress, Treasury Secretary Robert Anderson noted that "it showed the rich countries' commitment" to helping to meet the development needs of the poor nations and would help them "advance their economic life under free institutions."[31] For the United States it also provided a way to get other developed countries to begin to share more of what had come to be seen as the aid burden. As in the case of the IFC, the International Development Association received strong support from a broad range of national groups, and legislation authorizing U.S. participation passed both houses of Congress by comfortable margins. As had been recommended in the advisory board report a decade earlier, the United States assumed a substantial (42 percent) share of the initial IDA contribution and took the lead in mobilizing the support of other countries.

The End of an Era

With the establishment of the IDA, the start-up phase of what came to be known as the World Bank was complete. Having led in this launching, the United States over the next decade encouraged the Bank to expand its lending to low-income countries, become more involved in addressing the need for increases in agricultural productivity and other major emerging development problems, and take the lead in approaching politically sensitive matters such as trade and industrial liberalization in India. Although disagreements arose between the U.S. government and the World Bank in the 1960s that tested the Bank's autonomy, for the most part relations were good. The United States was still by far the dominant member country. Its bilateral aid program remained for a time the larger and more innovative force in the enterprise of development assistance, and in many cases it worked closely with the Bank in the field. The professional development community, which emerged largely in the United States, also gave intellectual support to the strategy of development advanced by the United States and the Bank.

The support for the buildup of the Bank's development financing formed part of a U.S. turn to long-term economic development assistance in the 1950s and early 1960s. Although the early geographic focus of economic aid to the third world was a few countries in East Asia, by 1960 assistance had been expanded. The poverty-ridden countries of South Asia, America's near neighbors in Latin America, and later the emerging independent states of Africa all became recipients under a program of assistance that was building in the late Eisenhower years and was expanded after President Kennedy took office in 1961.

The Soviet Union had by then developed nuclear weapons, launched Sputnik, and extended its diplomatic reach into Africa, Asia, and America's neighbor, Cuba. Out of concern that the developing countries would succumb to the influence of communist ideology and the offers of support from the Soviet Union, the Kennedy administration took steps to strengthen U.S. foreign assistance. It consolidated existing aid programs into the Agency for International Development (AID), created the Peace Corps and the Alliance for Progress, and emphasized the need for the transfer of large financial resources by both bilateral and multilateral institutions. The rationale for this new aid was based on the conviction that deterrence of the Soviet military threat, while a necessary keystone of U.S. foreign policy, was not in itself adequate. It was an essential American interest that the countries of the developing world achieve economic growth and social stability within a democratic framework, not only to limit the Soviet orbit of interest but also to avoid the evolution of those nations into authoritarian systems that would be anti-American and anti-Western. These goals were believed to require a program of economic development aid to foster self-sustaining growth; and to be effective, programs of assistance needed to be institutionally divorced from the foreign policy apparatus.[32]

Development activists in later years have looked back on this as a time of "high expectations ... both in the United States and in the Third World ... [and] the only time when a true national consensus in favor of active development cooperation with the Third World prevailed." The consensus "brought together those motivated by security concerns . . . [and] those motivated by humanitarianism and a belief in the United States' interest in a rapidly expanding . . . world economy."[33] But the consensus proved short-lived.

In the context of the Kennedy administration's expanded foreign assistance policy, the United States took the lead in the first replenishment negotiations for IDA, calling for support of the Bank president's request for a fivefold, $1.5 billion three-year funding increase and seeking a reduction in the U.S. share from its initial 42.34 percent to 33.3 percent. In the face of resistance from other donors, however, it settled for a smaller replenishment (of $750 million) and only a token reduction in the share (41.89 percent). The IDA 2 negotiations were far more troubled, however.[34] IDA, as distinct from the World Bank itself, required the use of tax dollars and, with the second replenishment, became the lightening rod of U.S. World Bank policy.

George Woods became president of the Bank in 1963, taking over from Eugene Black. Woods was also a New York banker, but unlike his predecessor, he did not retain control over the appointment of the U.S. executive director, nor were relations between him and the U.S. government as close and as congenial as Black's had been. The change in relations had partly to do with personality.[35] But it had far more to do with changing U.S. economic fortunes and domestic policy concerns. The change was evident in the role the United States took in the IDA 2 negotiations. Although it had taken the lead in promoting the first IDA replenishment, when negotiations began on IDA 2, the United States was committed to reducing its outflow of dollars, resisting inflation, and maintaining the integrity (preventing a devaluation) of the dollar.[36]

Henry Fowler, secretary of the Treasury, urged Woods to lead the IDA 2 negotiations if he wanted to expand the agency. Woods proposed a $1 billion replenishment, which the United States favored. Concerned with avoiding a negative effect on its own balance of payments, however, the United States pressed hard in the negotiations for special balance of payments safeguards and a significant reduction in its IDA share, an objective that was to be emphasized in all subsequent replenishments. The United States did not gain agreement on either the "tied" or burden-sharing arrangements it sought, but it did achieve special "end of the queue" treatment for its contribution.

Even with that concession, however, congressional debate on IDA 2 questioned so large an increase at a time when government was cutting domestic programs and raising taxes. The debate delayed approval of U.S. participation, leaving other countries to advance funding to avoid a temporary suspension in IDA lending. In 1966 in response to the difficulty that foreign aid in general and the IDA negotiations in particular had begun to face in the United States, Woods hired a retired U.S. senator, A. Willis Robertson, to serve as consultant and lobbyist. By the time the IDA 2 negotiations were completed and brought to Congress for approval, Robert McNamara had become Bank president. The difficulty he faced in getting IDA 2 approved led him to take the further step of assigning to a senior Bank staff member, William Clark, the responsibility of building and maintaining better communications with Congress.[37] In sum, with the second replenishment, a pattern of U.S. demands for concessions and delays in authorizing or appropriating its IDA contributions had emerged. By the end of the 1960s the era of innovative and active U.S. leadership in development had begun to wane.

Policy Evolution and Erosion of Support

Three main objectives guided U.S. policy toward the Bank in the 1950s and early 1960s. The first was to build a strong organization as a means of promoting the stability and growth of a free and open world economy. The second was to ease the burden on the United States of providing economic assistance to other countries by leveraging funds from the private market and, with their recovery from World War II, from other industrialized countries. The third was to support countries of importance to the United States. Although these were to remain major objectives, during the 1970s U.S. support for and leadership in the Bank faltered.

The United States had launched the Bank in a foreign policy environment different from the one that emerged in the early 1970s. Three changes proved to have major bearing on relations between the United States and the Bank.

The first was the relative decline of the United States in the world economy. By 1973 the U.S. share of world GDP had shrunk to 26 percent from a level of nearly 35 percent two decades earlier.[38] Western Europe and Japan grew more rapidly through the 1960s than did the United States, which also experienced a shift from persistent balance of payments surplus, with resultant dollar shortages in the rest of the world, to frequent deficits. The postwar economic boom had also given way to concerns about domestic poverty, unemployment, and race inequalities. The 1971 dollar devaluation and general deterioration in the country's economic situation turned attention to the costs of U.S. international economic policy. As spelled out by a Treasury official in 1972,

> There is a . . . sharply heightened feeling in the United States today that the economic interests of our country have not been given sufficient weight in international policy making. What follows from this is that financial and other burdens traditionally accepted without question by the United States can no longer be automatically accepted on that basis. The new international economic environment is radically different from the familiar "post-war" period that must now be regarded as definitively ended. Now, the United States is compelled to weigh its actions in terms of the benefits and the burdens that will result.[39]

A second change for the country was the Vietnam War and the shattering of the foreign aid constituency. The prolonged and divisive war provoked domestic dissent and uncertainty about the U.S. role in the world. One observer commented, "virtually all the familiar geopolitical moorings of U.S. foreign policy have become unhitched. What for years seemed axiomatic now seems dubious, if not false. John F. Kennedy may be the last President who could, without creating a credibility gap, maintain that 'we in this country . . . are—by destiny rather than choice—the watchmen on the walls of world freedom.'"[40] The policy of containment, that had shaped U.S. activities in the developing world in the 1950s and early 1960s "was progressively abandoned in the late 1960s and 1970s, less because of a national consensus that the Soviet threat had declined than because of a sense that the Vietnam experience demonstrated that such a policy, when severely tested, was excessively expensive and not necessarily effective."[41] Moreover, the Agency for International Development, which had been heavily involved in Vietnam, was seriously discredited. Although it maintained considerable programmatic energy into the mid-1970s, both it and foreign assistance generally lost their solid constituency.

Changes in perspectives on development further shattered the coalition of support for foreign aid, including support for the World Bank. In the early 1970s, development experts and public interest development groups began to criticize the prevailing trickle-down theory of development. Despite McNamara's efforts to broaden the lending policy of the Bank, the institution came under attack for supporting regimes that were persistent violators of human rights and for not doing enough to aid the poor. Constituency groups, which had given nearly automatic support to U.S. funding of the Bank, became at best conditional proponents. The problem was worsened by the rapid growth of lending under the dynamic leadership of McNamara, which stimulated a considerable increase in public and congressional attention to Bank policies and practices.

A final change was the onset of congressional activism in foreign policy. The creation of IDA, with its requirement for regular replenishments, brought Congress into the making of U.S. policy toward the Bank in a significant way. Before the early 1970s Congress's role was a relatively passive one, certainly as compared to its involvement with the bilateral aid program. It had strongly supported the launching of the Bank and the establishment of the two early Bank affiliates. But for the most part, early congressional action consisted of approving administration requests for U.S. membership in the Bank and providing funding for it. Although individual members raised particular concerns from time to time in private exchanges with the executive branch or Bank management, their public statements usually supported administration policy. This pattern began to change in the 1960s when support for foreign aid waned and Congress dragged its feet on the first and second IDA replenishments. It was the changes of the late 1960s and early 1970s, however, that led to an increasing activism on the part of Congress. Since then, Congress has used its power of the purse to direct and restrict U.S. participation in the Bank in many specific ways.[42]

The development that contributed most to Congress's more active role was the growth in the Bank's lending program and the corresponding increase of administration funding requests, especially for IDA. According to the Bank's annual reports, appropriations for all multilateral development banks rose in nominal terms from $700 million in fiscal year 1970 to $2.3 billion in fiscal year 1980. This increase attracted the attention of Congress, the press, and the development policy constituency in the United States. Although the Bank regularly fared better in Congress from the 1970s on than did other multilateral agencies or the bilateral aid program, the increases in appropriation requests provoked much greater scrutiny and heightened criticism of policies and practices. Although most of the criticism came from traditional opponents of foreign aid, from the 1970s on, prodevelopment groups, including mainly church groups and private voluntary organizations, began to lobby in opposition to an ever widening range of specific features of Bank operations. Previously the active bulwarks of support, these groups became provisional proponents willing to endorse U.S. contributions to the Bank only if certain reforms were made in its policies and practices.

Foreign aid has never been popular in Congress. Although objections were muted in the years just after World War II, Congress quickly became dissatisfied with it and distrustful of multilateral institutions. No one ever ran for Congress on a pro-aid platform nor got elected for supporting the World Bank. As a consequence, most members of Congress were uninterested and uninformed about the Bank's operations. Even on key committees there has been much misunderstanding of what the Bank did and how it operated.[43] Executive branch leadership and active constituency groups provided the initial energy and pressure to sustain support; but with both in decline by the 1970s, the increased appropriation requests became attractive targets.

Two other forces, unrelated to the Bank's performance, were at work as well. The Vietnam War not only shattered the consensus on foreign policy but also ended the period of congressional quiescence on foreign affairs. Many members of Congress deeply objected to the escalation of U.S. involvement in the war and to the Johnson and Nixon administrations' attempts to use bilateral and multilateral aid in support of the war effort. As a consequence, Congress sought a greater role in directing foreign policy, which included more detailed oversight of U.S. participation in the Bank.

At the same time, there was a breakdown of discipline and effective leadership in Congress that made it infinitely more difficult to maneuver unpopular aid requests through the labyrinthine authorization and appropriation procedures. No fewer than five committees came to have significant jurisdiction over policy toward the Bank. This arrangement provided multiple entry points for interested groups with specific policy agendas, and it created the opportunity for strategically placed members of Congress and specific issues to gain disproportionate weight in the policy process. As long as Congress was passive in making Bank policy, its basic dislike of foreign aid and multilateral institutions and its cumbersome legislative procedures were of limited significance. But as it became less deferential on matters of foreign affairs, these factors became formative influences on U.S. policy toward and participation in the Bank.

A number of studies written in the late 1960s and early 1970s urged the United States to increase its reliance on multilateral assistance as a way to counter growing "aid fatigue" and improve the effectiveness of development assistance.[44] Although multilateral aid had increased fourfold under the Kennedy administration, it accounted for less than 10 percent of total U.S. foreign assistance at the end of the 1960s. The proposals for a shift in favor of multilateral aid were based on several rationales. Because waning public support for foreign aid would not allow the United States to continue to increase its foreign aid program, the multilateral development banks offered the best means of leveraging funds for developing countries. By relying on multilateral institutions to promote effective development policies, the United States could depoliticize foreign assistance and avoid strains in its relations with developing countries that resulted from bilateral policy interference. Finally, the multilateral development banks could promote more coordination and fewer unproductive and costly overlaps in international aid efforts.[45] The recommendation was picked up by the incoming Nixon administration, and in a message submitted to Congress in September 1970, President Nixon proposed a sweeping reorganization of the U.S. bilateral aid program and greater reliance on multilateral aid. The United States, he said, "should channel an increasing share of its development assistance through multilateral institutions as readily as practicable. . . . Our remaining bilateral assistance should be provided largely within a framework established by the international institutions."[46]

However, the relative increase in U.S. multilateral development bank contributions occurred in the mid-1960s and, in real terms, has held fairly steady since then (table 2). Thus its relative share of total U.S. foreign aid has reflected more the ebb and flow of bilateral aid levels, not any real increase in the proportion of U.S. aid flows through multilateral institutions in the 1970s or thereafter.

In fact, a substantial deterioration occurred in U.S. relations with the World Bank during the 1970s. This change was marked by frequent open conflict between the two over a variety of issues, repeated failures on the part of the United States to deliver on its share of replenishments within the same period as other member countries and, by the end of the decade, the breakdown of the bipartisanship in U.S. Bank policy that had prevailed since the signing of the Bretton Woods Act.

The Early 1970s

The early 1970s marked a turning point that began with a souring of relations between the Bank and the U.S. Treasury. As one indication of trouble, in early 1972 the United States gave "belated and grudging" support to Robert McNamara for a second term as World Bank president.[47] According to the press, McNamara was not the first choice of Republican President Nixon. Names of former Republican cabinet members were proposed, but the international development constituency came out strongly in McNamara's support, and European member states hinted that if the U.S. nominee were not McNamara, they might advance a European alternative.[48] According to a retrospective analysis of these years by the Bank's vice president for external affairs during his term, McNamara "had irritated many important leaders in the Nixon administration. They had thought that, as an American, McNamara should be responsive to policy nudges, but over and over again he proved to be unnudgeable."[49] The grudging support for his nomination was a harbinger of difficulties that beset his relations with the United States until Jimmy Carter's election to the presidency.

Also in 1971 at the initiative of the executive branch, the United States cast its first no vote on a World Bank loan. The proposed loan was to Guyana and was opposed by the United States as part of a policy condemning expropriation of U.S. private property. Although this was not the first credit the United States had opposed, it was the first time that it chose to cast an opposing vote on the Bank's executive board and thereby put its disagreement with the Bank on the record.

Two years later, in negotiations for the fourth IDA replenishment, the United States was for the first time the main donor country seeking to limit the increase in contributions. It made the World Bank and other countries take over its role of conciliator, soliciting contributions and arranging compromises. Moreover, it demanded and got a number of concessions. On the list of U.S. conditions for the replenishment were the establishment of an independent audit process for Bank operations, removal of the maintenance of value obligation that required member countries to maintain the foreign exchange values of their IDA contributions, and a commitment for a future leveling off of IDA

Table 2. U.S. Foreign Aid, by Major Programs, 1946–89
Billions of constant 1989 dollars

Year	Development assistance	Food aid	Other economic aid	Multi-lateral development banks	Economic support fund	Military aid	Total
1946	. . .	. . .	17.6	4.6	. . .	. . .	22.2
1947	. . .	. . .	39.6	. . .	. . .	1.0	40.6
1948	. . .	. . .	15.1	. . .	. . .	1.7	16.8
1949	33.3	. . .	8.2	. . .	. . .	1.6	43.1
1950	19.3	. . .	6.0	. . .	. . .	6.3	31.6
1951	12.5	. . .	3.9	. . .	0.8	21.2	38.4
1952	8.9	0.4	1.7	. . .	1.0	21.9	33.9
1953	7.4	. . .	1.4	. . .	2.1	13.3	24.2
1954	3.4	0.3	0.5	. . .	7.4	11.4	23.0
1955	2.8	2.5	0.1	. . .	6.0	7.9	19.3
1956	1.7	4.0	0.2	. . .	5.3	10.8	22.0
1957	2.3	5.1	0.2	0.2	5.0	8.6	21.4
1958	3.7	3.4	0.1	. . .	3.4	6.6	17.2
1959	4.5	3.5	0.1	. . .	3.6	9.5	21.2
1960	4.4	4.0	0.1	0.3	3.4	9.2	21.4
1961	5.2	4.6	0.1	0.3	3.4	8.5	22.1
1962	7.2	5.6	1.1	0.7	3.2	8.2	26.0
1963	7.1	5.6	1.1	0.5	2.4	7.9	24.6
1964	7.0	5.8	0.7	0.4	1.8	4.6	20.3
1965	6.4	5.1	1.0	1.2	1.8	4.9	20.4
1966	6.5	5.7	0.7	1.3	3.3	7.8	25.3
1967	5.8	3.4	0.6	1.3	2.7	8.5	22.2
1968	5.4	4.5	0.6	1.4	2.1	9.1	23.1
1969	4.0	3.8	0.6	1.6	1.4	10.1	21.5
1970	4.2	3.5	0.5	1.5	1.5	8.9	20.1

replenishments in real terms. The United States also demanded a commitment for a reduction in the differences between U.S. official and World Bank salaries and due consideration of the U.S. position in response to the expropriation of U.S. private property in Peru. In addition, it demanded and received a substantial reduction in its share of IDA funding and agreement on stretching out its contribution over four years rather than the regular three. These arrangements allowed the United States to hold its annual payment to the same level in current dollars as in

Table 2. (Continued)

Year	Develop- ment assistance	Food aid	Other economic aid	Multi- lateral develop- ment banks	Economic support fund	Military aid	Total
1971	3.7	3.6	0.5	0.5	1.7	12.8	22.8
1972	4.0	3.4	1.4	0.4	1.7	14.0	24.9
1973	3.6	2.9	0.6	2.0	1.6	14.1	24.8
1974	2.8	2.4	0.8	2.0	1.6	11.2	20.8
1975	2.9	2.9	0.6	1.7	2.7	4.4	15.2
1976	2.5	2.7	0.5	0.1	2.3	5.2	13.3
1976TQ	0.8	0.4	0.2	0.7	1.8	1.3	5.2
1977	2.7	2.3	0.5	1.8	3.3	4.1	14.7
1978	3.3	2.2	0.4	2.0	3.9	4.2	16.0
1979	3.0	2.1	0.6	2.7	3.2	11.0	22.6
1980	2.8	2.2	0.9	2.2	3.3	3.2	14.6
1981	2.7	2.1	0.8	1.3	3.0	4.6	14.5
1982	2.6	1.7	0.7	1.6	3.5	5.5	15.6
1983	2.7	1.7	0.6	1.8	3.6	6.9	17.3
1984	2.9	1.8	0.6	1.6	3.7	7.7	18.3
1985	3.2	2.3	0.7	1.8	6.0	6.6	20.6
1986	2.9	1.8	0.6	1.3	5.4	6.4	18.4
1987	2.3	1.5	0.7	1.6	3.8	5.5	15.4
1988 (est.)	2.3	1.6	0.7	1.5	3.3	5.6	15.0
1989 (req.)	2.2	1.4	0.6	1.5	3.3	5.6	14.6
Total	218.9	113.8	114.8	45.4	123.3	349.4	965.6

Source: Stanley J. Heginbotham and Larry Q. Knowles, *An Overview of U.S. Foreign Aid Programs* (Congressional Research Service, 1988), p. 17.

IDA 3, while other countries made sizable increases in their contributions.

In asserting the U.S. position on IDA 4, the Nixon administration clearly had one eye on mounting deficits and signs of inflation in the U.S. economy and one eye on Congress, which was becoming increasingly restless over various aspects of the administration's Bank policy. However, the major breakpoint in U.S. policy focused not on IDA but the Bank itself, and it was brought on not by Congress but by the executive branch, which voiced strong opposition to continued growth in lending. At the outset of the first oil shock in 1973–74, the United States expressed skepticism about continued expansion of regular Bank lending and opposed initial efforts by McNamara to enlist development funds from oil producers with capital surpluses. In early 1974 he sought agreement from those countries on establishing an OPEC fund for development whose operations would be carried out by existing World Bank staff and whose votes would be divided equally into three groups: OPEC, developed, and developing countries. "But he had reckoned without the determination of the Americans . . . to break the OPEC cartel and not to collaborate with it in any way. In the face of U.S. opposition the proposals sank without trace."[50] Recycling of petrodollars, the United States held, was a function best left to the commercial banks.

The success of OPEC in manipulating a fourfold increase in oil prices emboldened developing countries in the mid-1970s to intensify demands for a new international economic order. Acting in concert, they demanded a greater share of the benefits from international economic cooperation and a greater voice in the system. In staunchly opposing these demands the United States insisted on the need for developing countries to put their national economic policies in order and emphasized the importance of the Bretton Woods institutions in assisting development. In a speech written for the special session of the UN General Assembly in September 1975, which was intended to be responsive to but not supportive of the developing countries' demands, Secretary of State Henry Kissinger offered a number of initiatives, including two new facilities to be linked to the World Bank and U.S. support for expansion of both the IFC and the Bank.[51] Although these were initiatives that would have had a relatively small impact on the U.S. budget, the political strategy of the State Department was constrained by strong Treasury opposition to continued growth in World Bank lending.

In a dispute that came to a head at the annual meeting of the Bank in 1976, the Ford administration's Treasury secretary, William Simon, countered McNamara's call for increased Bank lending and an attendant general increase in the Bank's capital. Simon supported IDA but opposed the rate of the Bank's growth in both borrowing and lending. In contrast to McNamara's emphasis on the need for increased lending in the wake of the oil price hikes, declining global growth, and mounting third world debt, Simon called for a concerted attack on inflation at home and abroad and insisted that the time had come for deficit countries to slow their borrowing and for less developed countries to adjust their economic policies to allow for greater reliance on market forces. In his statement at the annual meeting Simon foreshadowed several issues that figured prominently in the policy of the Reagan administration.

In considering how the present system might be improved to the mutual benefit of all nations, we should be guided by the following principles:

——Development by definition is a long-term process. . . . Foreign aid can help, but such aid can only complement and supplement those policies developing countries adopt, which in the end will be decisive.

——The role of the private sector is critical. There is no substitute for a vigorous private sector mobilizing the resources and energies of the people of the developing countries.

——A market-oriented system is not perfect, but it is better than any alternative system. . . .

—A basic focus must be on increasing savings and making the institutional and policy improvements which will enable the financial markets to channel those savings into activities that enhance the opportunities for people to live better lives.[52]

Simon contended that the larger role McNamara sought for the Bank would result in some nations borrowing beyond their capacity to repay and would weaken the Bank's standing in the capital markets. He insisted, therefore, that Bank lending should be temporarily frozen at current levels. In IDA 5 negotiations the United States also expressed an unwillingness to see its annual payments increase. After other countries countered by insisting that it maintain a reasonable proportional share, negotiations concluded with an agreement on a smaller replenishment than had been proposed by the Bank. Thus the long-standing U.S. goal of burden sharing had come to have the effect of holding down rather than increasing IDA contributions.

In the view of senior Treasury officials, the Bank was out of control. According to the U.S. executive director, they were concerned that the rapid growth in lending, which had resulted in massive undispersed commitments, was mortgaging the Bank's future borrowing capacity and that Bank management was not responsive to donor criticism. Treasury also raised questions about the bankability of new projects undertaken as part of the Bank's emphasis on alleviating poverty and about the Bank's support for widening the role of governments in the development process.[53] To others in the Bank and on the executive board, however, U.S. opposition to the rapid growth of the Bank appeared to reflect two quite different concerns. First, with U.S. bilateral aid shrinking, a growing Bank might displace the U.S. economic, and therefore political, leverage in developing countries. Second, with the increase in Bank borrowing in non-U.S. markets, the United States would lose its influence over how and where Bank funds were spent. Opposition to an increase in the capital subscription of Japan, which would have eroded the U.S. veto, was taken as an indication of the latter concern.[54]

One effect of a policy less supportive of the Bank was that the United States fell behind in its contributions to the Bank and IDA. The delay eroded U.S. relations with other member countries, a problem the Carter administration sought to remedy later in the decade. But it had to contend with, and itself contributed to, the worst period in relations between the World Bank and Congress.

The Proliferation of Legislative Restrictions

By the time President Carter came to office, Congress had established a practice of tying directives to its approval of World Bank funding bills. These restrictions proliferated rapidly in the second half of the 1970s because of the personalities in key congressional positions, the growing criticism of the Bank from both liberal and conservative members of Congress, and the mismanagement of legislative relations by Carter administration officials.

The Foreign Operations Subcommittee of the House Appropriations Committee, which essentially held the House purse strings on foreign aid, was chaired from 1955 to 1977 by Otto Passman of Louisiana. Passman "voted against every foreign aid authorization after the 1947 Greek-Turkey loan and he gave the program a skeptical treatment during the twenty-two years he chaired the panel."[55] In 1977 Clarence Long of Maryland took over as chair. Although he was more supportive of the goals and purposes of the U.S. foreign aid program, he was generally critical of the World Bank. His criticism focused particularly on what he viewed as the Bank's failure to help the poor, but many have claimed that the death of his son in Vietnam made him a staunch and unrelenting critic of Robert McNamara and his tenure in office. The rise in congressional opposition to the Bank was not limited to Long and the subcommittee, however. It was fed by public interest groups on both the Left and the

Right and by increased coverage of the Bank in the media as each replenishment required larger funding bills.

Paradoxically, one effect of Congress's increased attention was to bring development issues more into focus in the formation of policy toward the Bank. In the 1950s and 1960s, when bilateral aid was the dominant force in development assistance, the United States interacted closely with the Bank in the field, and U.S. policy toward the Bank was mediated, to a considerable extent, by coordinated actions of the Bank and AID within countries. This interaction was especially intense in South Asia when the United States was giving large amounts of aid to India and Pakistan and in Latin America during the Alliance for Progress. Although the agencies continued to interact, by the mid-1970s AID had become a less innovative force in development. U.S. relations with the Bank were left largely to the Treasury and State Departments, which brought little development interest or expertise to policymaking. With no place in the executive branch to consider the development policies and performance of the Bank, the development community turned to Congress, which from the 1970s on showed more concern and interest in the effectiveness of development assistance programs than did the bureaucracy.

Congress's initiative in 1973 to set "new directions" for the U.S. aid program was a clear example of this interest.[56] Although the new directions legislation did not succeed in shoring up waning public support for foreign aid, it did set guidelines for the executive branch in the uses of aid dollars appropriated by Congress. In subsequent years Congress gave increasing attention to new directions issues in its deliberation of Bank funding bills. Thus in the late 1970s and throughout the 1980s, Congress held hearings, requested studies, and at times mandated that the United States use its voice and vote in the Bank to strengthen the development impact of Bank lending, particularly in alleviating poverty.

The interest of some members of Congress in development was not sufficient, however, to withstand the general waning of support for foreign aid and growing attacks on the Bank from both traditional opponents and proponents of foreign aid. As a result, the effort of securing money for the Bank came to dominate policymaking.

Congressional reluctance to appropriate funds for the Bank mounted. This reluctance led, first, to delays in voting the full amount of funding requested by the executive branch, and the United States failed repeatedly to deliver its shares of negotiated replenishments on time. One of the most dramatic instances of this was the 1974 defeat of the IDA 4 funding bill in the House. Although Congress had held up approval of the first three IDA funding requests, the IDA 4 bill was the first to be defeated. The action was taken in a burst of anger over the economy and was actually less an indication of Congress's attitude toward the Bank than of a general discontent in the wake of Watergate, oil price hikes, and stagflation. Although the action was successfully overturned in a later vote after heavy administration lobbying, the defeat clearly demonstrated a new vulnerability of Bank funding requests. In subsequent years Congress not only delayed making appropriations but also, from time to time, appropriated less, sometimes far less, than the amounts requested by the executive branch and less than what was required to meet pledges made by the United States in international negotiations. As a consequence, the United States became the only donor to fall into arrears to the Bank.

In this environment, "particularism . . . found fertile soil."[57] In effect, Congress became the staging ground for criticisms of the Bank that multiplied as funding requests grew larger. More and more, committee chairs had to cater to members' particularistic views to obtain the support necessary to move authorization and appropriation bills. Vocal minorities exacted concessions on an array of narrow, short-run issues, or committee bills were altered by floor amendments proposed with little regard for their ultimate impact on the operations of the Bank. In the absence of a strong constituency that could be mobilized by the floor leadership to counter particularistic amendments, an extensive body of legislation built up that required the United States to go to the Bank and seek numerous specific concessions.

Many of the issues that were built into legislation were brought to Congress by outside groups, but not all. One of the first issue-specific legislative actions was the Gonzalez amendment of 1972, which required the United States to oppose World Bank loans to countries that had expropriated U.S. private investments without proper compensation.58 In the 1960s Congress had passed legislation barring U.S. bilateral aid to countries that confiscated U.S. investments (the 1962 Hickenlooper amendment) and requiring the United States to vote against Inter-American Development Bank loans to them. The 1972 legislation extended the restriction to loans of all multilateral development banks. The World Bank, at U.S. urging, had adopted operational guidelines in response to expropriations, and the administration had sought to discourage expropriations through a variety of diplomatic efforts, but the Gonzalez amendment overruled a reluctance within the bureaucracy to adopt a formal, blanket statement of opposition.[59]

Although expropriation policy was the specific issue, support for the amendment was driven by a broader concern with Congress's role in the oversight of U.S. aid policy. Having increased its control over the bilateral aid program through various legislative restrictions and earmarkings, Congress was unwilling to see its directives circumvented by the relative increase in multilateral aid that the administration sought at the start of the 1970s. As a House Appropriations Committee report stated in 1972,

> The Committee is deeply concerned over the trend to direct an increasing amount of U.S. foreign assistance through the multilateral institutions while at the same time decreasing the bilateral aid program. . . . The same degree of detailed examination which is possible in the bilateral foreign assistance programs is not possible in the multilateral assistance programs. The Congress does not know when, where or how the budget requests will be disbursed by these multilateral organizations because they do not justify their requests by specific project.[60]

This broader concern was repeatedly voiced in subsequent years, with attention focused on the inadequacy of executive branch consultation with Congress, the need for more information from the Bank, and the need for more independent and more transparent evaluation and audit procedures. At Congress's request the General Accounting Office undertook several assessments of the management of U.S. Bank policy and the evaluation and audit procedures.61 On the basis of a 1978 report, Congress passed legislation directing the United States to establish an independent review mechanism. But the reforms that followed did little to quiet the charge that the executive branch was using support for the multilateral development banks as a way around congressional restrictions on bilateral aid and that the Bank was unresponsive to Congress's requests for more information and more transparency. A Senate report said in 1978, "for more than five years the Committee has pressed the banks to open their doors and encourage both their supporters and the media to make informed judgments as to how well and how efficiently they are carrying out their international mandate. It is apparent that our exhortations have fallen on deaf ears."[62] Criticism was even more strongly worded in a House minority report that same year: "By making our contributions through multilateral institutions, Congress has lost the ability to have control over how American tax dollars are spent and who will receive them. . . . The fact that the administration wants to put even more of these tax dollars into multilateral aid programs will remove even further the oversight capability of the Congress."[63] And in 1979, under the leadership of Clarence Long, the House Appropriations Committee issued an investigative report that strongly criticized the ability of the United States to influence the Bank, the inadequacy of audit and evaluation systems, the limited flow of information to Congress and the public, and the Bank's record on lending to the poor.[64]

In addition to congressional oversight and Bank transparency, five other issues dominated congressional debate through the 1970s and into the 1980s (there were many more). Through successive pieces of legislation, these matters became demands that the government was instructed to pursue within the Bank.

MANAGEMENT AND PERSONNEL PRACTICES. Congress's attitude that the Bank was excessively closed and arrogant was inflamed by the high Bank staff salaries and the difficulties Congress encountered in getting information on them. Whether or not the issue was deliberately fanned by those opposed to foreign aid, and particularly multilateral aid, it seriously undermined Hill support for the Bank. A Senate subcommittee report commented in 1975, "many who are said to be dedicated servants of the poor receive unseemly compensation for their service."[65] A year later Congress indicated that future IDA appropriations would be affected by progress on reducing salaries, and the following year it adopted legislation directing the administration to seek to keep Bank and IMF salaries and benefits at levels comparable to those paid by private employers and the U.S. government. Subsequently, the Bank and the IMF agreed to personnel guidelines that closely followed a U.S. proposal to set salary schedules by reference to a basket of compensation packages of civil servants of several member governments and the U.S. private sector.[66] This action reduced the level of controversy for a time, but it did not eliminate the salary issue. In 1989 Congress recommended that the Treasury make known to the Bank its "extreme displeasure" with a salary increase and "the damaging impact such a large increase has on support for the World Bank in Congress."[67]

LENDING TO SPECIFIC COUNTRIES. Before the mid-1970s, Congress voiced little concern over World Bank country allocations, with the notable exception lending to countries that expropriated U.S. private property. After the mid-1970s, however, Congress frequently expressed opposition to loans to particular countries. India was an early target of criticism, and support in Congress for IDA replenishments was undermined by India's large share of IDA resources, which exceeded 40 percent at its peak. Legislation targeted particularly at India instructed the U.S. representative in the Bank to consider whether a recipient country had detonated a nuclear device or refused to sign the Treaty on Non-proliferation of Nuclear Weapons. And in response to congressional pressure the administration made the reduction of India's share a condition of IDA negotiations. More controversial and more strident was a late 1970s effort, led by Representative Bill Young, to stop lending to Vietnam and five other socialist countries. Young and other conservative members of Congress strongly objected to what they viewed as the Bank's support of socialist regimes and statist solutions to development problems. Young believed that indirect U.S. aid to Vietnam through multilateral development banks was especially objectionable, and his opposition led to a major dispute over a proposed earmarking of U.S. contributions to the Bank.

PROTECTION OF U.S. PRODUCERS. From 1976 through the 1980s, Congress also objected to Bank lending to increase the production of commodities that could compete with U.S. commodities. In 1977 Congress adopted legislation requiring U.S. executive directors at each of the multilateral development banks to oppose loans for the production of palm oil, citrus crops, and sugar.[68] In 1978, Congress mandated U.S. directors' opposition to all loans for the production of export commodities, including mineral commodities, that were in surplus in world markets and that could cause substantial injury to U.S. producers.[69] Proposed but not passed was a more stringent amendment to the 1987 omnibus trade act that sought to prohibit the United States from participating in future funding agreements for multilateral development banks that made loans for the production of agricultural and mineral commodities in surplus in the world market. And in 1989 Congress extended its legislative restrictions by mandating the U.S. executive director to vote against loans that would subsidize development of export industries in countries engaging in dumping or other unfair practices against the United States.

AID TO THE POOR. Consistent with the new directions policy, Congress also mandated that the United States pressure the Bank to increase the share of its assistance going to the poor and expand its emphasis on projects designed to meet basic human needs. Despite recognition of the efforts made under the leadership of Robert McNamara, both supporters and opponents of the Bank expressed a strong sense of frustration over the lack of assistance to the poor in the late 1970s, charges leveled mostly by liberal and conservative development groups. In the 1980s Congress forced renewed U.S. emphasis on alleviating poverty when it requested studies on the effects on poverty of structural adjustment and urged the administration to make attention to poverty alleviation a condition of its continuing support for IDA.

HUMAN RIGHTS. In 1975 an effort by Representative Tom Harkin led to a provision requiring the U.S. representative to the Inter-American and African Development Banks to vote against loans to any country whose government violated its citizens' human rights. In 1976, although it lacked legislation covering World Bank lending, members of Congress nonetheless sought to persuade the administration to vote against Bank loans to Chile because of its human rights violations. But the Ford administration, wary of the effects of introducing human rights criteria into Bank lending decisions and convinced that it could not rally enough votes of other member countries to prevent the loans to Chile, voted in favor. In response, key members of Congress decided to enact new human rights legislation in the subsequent Congress, and a legislative battle ensued with the Carter administration.

The Failed Efforts of the Carter Administration

The Carter administration entered office committed to expanding U.S. development assistance, eliminating the arrearages that had built up in its payments to the multilateral development banks, and making the banks the keystone of U.S. development policy. Its support for the banks was clearly reflected by Michael Blumenthal in his confirmation hearings for Treasury secretary:

I would hope that to the largest extent possible, whatever we do as a country with regard to economic assistance be handled through multilateral organizations where we can be one of a group of countries who work together and contribute to the solution of these problems.

I think that the time for a large national program or a bilateral program for economic aid is probably past, except in certain exceptional circumstances. I expect our work in these international organizations to be very intense and very active.[70]

A report issued in the administration's first year further set the tone of its development assistance policy by calling for efforts to improve conditions in poor countries through economic and technical assistance, funds for meeting basic human needs, and increased multilateral lending.[71] This orientation was reiterated by President Carter in summit statements and in the congressional testimonies of Treasury and State Department officials. The administration immediately tried to win support for IDA funding and for the general capital increase that the Ford administration had opposed.

The Carter administration was beleaguered, however, by deteriorating economic conditions at home and abroad and, late in its term, by a consuming concern with the Iran hostage taking and Soviet expansionism in Afghanistan. As a result, despite its encouragement of the multilateral development banks and its close relations with McNamara, it was unable to build a political constituency for its development bank policies.[72] A concerted effort succeeded in convincing Congress to appropriate in a single package funds for the last payment of IDA 4 and the first of IDA 5. This action put the United States back on the same schedule as other donors, but it also meant that the IDA appropriation crossed the $1 billion mark for the first time. To sweeten the package, the Carter administration took on the contentious issue of World Bank salaries that had first been raised in the early 1970s. While indicating that it supported both the IDA funding and the general capital increase for the Bank, the administration informed the Bank and its board that it would not take a formal position on refunding until the compensation issue was resolved. Thus in 1978 the United States made a proposal to the Joint Committee on Compensation of the Bank and the Fund that, after much debate, became the basis of an across-the-board salary cut and the guideline for future salary increases. The U.S. formula did not, however, resolve the salary issue, which remained a major irritant in relations between the United States and the Bank and one of a growing number of matters emphasized by an increasingly hostile Congress.

VIETNAM AND THE DISPUTE OVER EARMARKING. Congress and the Carter administration came into their greatest conflict in a dispute over

Bank lending to Vietnam and an attempt by members of Congress to earmark U.S. contributions. The opposition was led by an alliance of liberal human rights activists and conservative opponents of foreign aid.

In its early days the Carter administration spoke of human rights as a centerpiece of its foreign policy. But like previous administrations, it sought to limit proposed legislation to a requirement that the United States use its voice to advance human rights concerns in countries that were borrowers of the Bank rather than use its vote to oppose loans to countries defined by the United States as violators of basic rights. Although human rights activists in Congress were willing to give the Carter administration the flexibility it sought, a coalition of the most active rights proponents in the House and conservative opponents of the development banks won passage of a provision that mandated the United States to vote no on loans, those except for meeting basic human needs, to any country with a poor human rights record.

In the midst of this debate an even more restrictive amendment was proposed by Representative Bill Young that sought to prohibit U.S. funds from being used for multilateral development bank loans to various socialist countries, including Vietnam and Uganda. Such earmarking had become a common practice with the bilateral aid program, but until the debate over supporting human rights, Congressional activism on MDB issues had mainly taken the form of cuts in appropriations and instructions to Treasury to use the U.S. voice and vote in the Bank to advance certain positions. Had the Young amendment become law, the Bank would have had to refuse the U.S. contribution because its charter prohibited it from accepting earmarked funds. To break congressional deadlock and to avoid having its total foreign aid request put into a continuing resolution with funding levels far short of what was being sought, the Carter administration struck a compromise with Young. In a letter to Congress, President Carter promised that the U.S. directors would vote against all MDB loans to the countries in question.[73] His promise did not, however, end the earmarking debate.

In 1978, over a U.S. objection, the Bank board approved a $60 million IDA loan to Vietnam for agricultural development. In response, the House of Representatives approved an amendment to its fiscal year 1979 appropriation bill that prohibited U.S. funds from being used for loans to Vietnam and several other countries. This action "served to place moderate members opposed to earmarking in the uncomfortable position of having to go on record opposing a measure to halt aid to Vietnam." Although the amendment was ultimately defeated in House-Senate conference, Young introduced a similar one in 1979 that led to heated debate on the Senate floor between conservatives in favor and moderate Democrats who supported the administration's stand against earmarking. Again the amendment went to conference, where it gave rise to "the most acrimonious foreign aid debate of the 1970s."[74]

At that point, McNamara took the unusual step of meeting with twelve members of Congress to assure them that a lending freeze had been imposed on Vietnam. But Young refused to back down until McNamara sent a letter to Congress stating that because of "a very serious question" about Vietnam's commitment to a rational development policy, there would be no new IDA loans to the country in the coming year.[75] Although the McNamara letter temporarily ended the earmarking conflict, the debate over aid to Vietnam reduced congressional support for the Bank to an all-time low and contributed significantly to shattering the tradition of bipartisanship on MDB policy.

BIPARTISANSHIP SHATTERED. Until the late 1970s, partisan divisions were not a major factor in congressional deliberations of U.S. Bank policy.[76] Democratic members of the House tended to vote in larger majorities for Bank bills than did their Republican counterparts, but the differences were not dramatic. Many members from both parties often voted in favor or against administration funding requests and a majority of Republicans often supported World Bank legislation.

Beginning in 1978, however, a series of highly critical minority reports were issued as part of the annual House Appropriations subcommittee report on foreign assistance. Then in 1980 Republicans made clear that they were prepared to oppose enactment of the large development bank funding bill proposed by the outgoing Carter administration. That same year the Republican presidential platform statement strongly emphasized bilateral rather than multilateral aid. Furthermore, in 1978 and again in 1980 legislative decisions on multilateral development banks became issues of electoral politics. Some Democratic incumbents were attacked by their opponents for allegedly supporting aid to Vietnam when they voted against the MDB earmarking amendments. Because the attacks appeared about the same time and in the same words in different parts of the country, the Democrats concluded that the Republican national electoral organizations had orchestrated the effort.[77] In response, Representative David Obey demanded that the incoming Reagan administration issue a statement opposing such attacks, and the House Democratic leadership told the new administration that it would have to mobilize more Republican support for future MDB legislation if the Democrats were to join in.[78] The Democrats held to this on a major funding bill that the Reagan administration, in its early days, had to bring to Congress as a piece of unfinished business of the Carter administration.

At the end of the decade the Carter administration entered into negotiations for both a sixth replenishment of IDA and a further capital increase for the World Bank. As it had done in 1977, it sought major concessions that it hoped would help win congressional approval for the refunding agreements. In the negotiation for a capital increase, the United States pressed to lower to 7.5 percent the amount of the increase that was to be paid in. It also insisted on further reducing the U.S. capital share and, in opposition to all other member countries, refused to accept the obligation to maintain the value of its commitments to the Bank against foreign exchange fluctuations. In the IDA 6 negotiations the United States made additional demands. Although it endorsed an increase, it again insisted on a smaller share and an increase in the roster of donors. Allowing for inflation, its pledge was thus the same as it had been for IDA 5. In addition, it demanded that the Bank increase lending for energy production and poverty alleviation projects, introducing into the IDA negotiations policy issues that other member countries viewed as in the purview of the board. The outcome was a substantial broadening of burden sharing but also a further fraying of U.S. relations with Bank management and other member countries.

Even with these concessions, lack of enthusiasm in Congress for the negotiated funding package and inept handling by the administration of the request to Congress delayed action on the replenishments. As a result the Carter administration left office recommending, but not having attained, adoption of the largest MDB package ever put before Congress, including $12 billion for the Bank and IDA combined. It also left U.S. policy toward MDBs in shambles. Despite its pro-Bank orientation, the administration had sought to achieve a multiplicity of objectives that it could not reconcile into a coherent and compelling strategy. Instead, in an effort to patch together the necessary margin of support for continued U.S. contributions to the Bank, the administration firmly established a practice of tying policy demands to replenishment agreements. In the aftermath of its election defeat, the Carter administration reached agreement with the incoming Reagan administration on a mutually acceptable, but not strong, nominee for McNamara's successor as president of the Bank; but it had to leave an unfinished agenda to a new administration, key members of which were openly critical of multilateral assistance.[79]

Retrenchment and Reassessment under Reagan

The Reagan administration came into office in January 1981 critical of the World Bank and other multilateral institutions on both ideological and political grounds and in favor of reduced U.S. support for them. This position represented a breakpoint in U.S. policy toward the Bank in two regards: previous Bank policy goals had been largely bipartisan in character, and disputes on specific issues notwithstanding, all previous administrations had supported the Bank as an important instrument of U.S. policy.

The 1980 Republican platform statement described America as dangerously adrift in a perilous world.

> Our country moves agonizingly, aimlessly, almost helplessly into one of the most dangerous and disorderly periods in history. . . . At home, our economy careens, whiplashed from one extreme to another. . . . Overseas, conditions already perilous, deteriorate. The Soviet Union for the first time is acquiring the means to obliterate or cripple our land-based missile system and blackmail us into submission. Marxist tyrannies spread more rapidly through the Third World and Latin America. Our alliances are frayed in Europe and elsewhere. Our energy supplies become even more dependent on uncertain foreign suppliers. In the ultimate humiliation, militant terrorists in Iran continue to toy with the lives of Americans.

The platform promised dramatic changes in U.S. foreign policy, including a return to bilateral assistance programs "whenever possible." Bilateral programs, it stated, "provide the best assurance that aid programs will be fully accountable to the American taxpayer, and wholly consistent with our foreign policy interests." It also criticized the Carter administration for diminishing the role of military assistance and foreign arms sales and pledged to "reform and rebuild" the military assistance programs.[80]

Immediately following the 1980 election, the new administration signaled its intentions not only to emphasize bilateral over multilateral programs and security over development assistance but also to seek a substantial reduction in foreign aid. This position was set out by the director of the Office of Management and Budget, David Stockman, in a planning memo leaked to the press on January 27, 1981, which called for a "foreign aid retrenchment." In his own account of the memo, Stockman described its rationale and objectives:

> The Gramm-Stockman budget plan had called for deep cuts in foreign economic aid on the basis of pure ideological principle. Both Gramm and I believed that the organs of international aid and so-called Third World development . . . were infested with socialist error. The international aid bureaucracy was turning Third World countries into quagmires of self-imposed inefficiency and burying them beneath mountainous external debts they would never be able to pay.[81]

Stockman also maintained that if Congress was to be persuaded to make cuts in domestic programs to achieve a balanced budget, aid increases of the size that had been proposed by the Carter administration would be out of the question. The memo proposed, therefore, to cut U.S. bilateral and multilateral aid by 45 percent, which would have amounted to a $13 billion reduction for 1982–86. The proposal would have revoked the U.S. pledge to contribute $3.2 billion to IDA 6 and reopened negotiations with other IDA donors to cut contributions in half. It would also have terminated all future U.S. contributions to IDA and the other multilateral development bank soft loan windows, frozen contributions to all UN agencies, held bilateral development assistance to no more than 3 percent growth while increasing the relative share of military assistance, and phased out both the Peace Corps and the P.L. 480 food credit sales program.

Strong State Department pressure blocked OMB and Treasury Department inclinations to renege on the Bank and IDA commitments that had been negotiated by the Carter administration. However, in agreeing to meet the commitments, the Reagan administration moved to advance its own policy perspectives. In its request to Congress for funds for IDA 6, it proposed a schedule of appropriations—$500 million in year one, $800 million in year two, and $1.8 billion in the third year—that it knew

Congress would not accept without stretching out the U.S. payment over four years.[82] The administration also made clear in its statements to Congress that its support for IDA 6 and a general capital increase should not be taken as a signal of future funding policies. It would, it announced, undertake a broad reassessment that would establish policy guidelines and a budgetary framework for U.S. participation in the multilateral development banks in the 1980s. Representative Jack Kemp, a staunch critic of foreign aid and IDA, then led the effort to line up support for the administration's 1981 World Bank request, organizing conservative Republican votes for IDA in exchange for Democratic support for bilateral military assistance.

The assessment that was subsequently undertaken was led by the Treasury Department.[83] It entailed an account of the role of the multilateral development banks in the international economic system, a review of criticisms of the banks over the years, and an evaluation of the ability of the United States to achieve its objectives through the banks. It also outlined a plan to improve MDB policy effectiveness and provided specific U.S. funding and policy recommendations. Although it discussed nineteen criticisms leveled against the banks, ranging from excessive salaries to support for statist development approaches to emphasis on loan quantity instead of quality, its tone was positive. To the surprise of many, the assessment approved the overall performance of the MDBs and noted the benefits to the United States of participation in them.

The main policy conclusions were not, however, wholly consistent with the body of the report. There were three core recommendations. First, U.S. support for the MDBs should be designed to foster greater adherence to open markets and greater emphasis on the private sector as the main vehicle for growth. Second, the United States should work to ensure that loan allocations were made conditional on policy reforms in recipient countries. Finally, the United States should reduce its expenditures on the banks. This third recommendation, the report suggested, should be accomplished in two ways. The United States should develop a plan to reduce and eventually phase out new paid-in capital for the hard loan windows of all MDBs. And it should reduce, in real terms, its future participation in all MDB soft loan windows, especially IDA. In other words, countries should be encouraged not only to adopt more market-based policies but also to rely more on private sector financing than on World Bank and other public sector financing.

The international debt crisis that burst onto the international stage not long after the Treasury assessment was completed required the Reagan administration to revise its views on graduating countries out of the ranks of World Bank borrowers. But it did not dampen the administration's criticism of the MDBs nor its own pressure for more focus on the private sector. In September 1983 President Reagan addressed the annual meeting of the World Bank and reiterated the policy directives contained in the Treasury report.

The societies that achieved the most spectacular, broad-based economic progress in the shortest period of time have not been the biggest in size, nor the richest in resources and certainly not the most rigidly controlled. What has united them all was their belief in the magic of the marketplace. Millions of individuals making their own decisions in the marketplace will always allocate resources better than any centralized government planning process.[84]

He also expressed the willingness of the United States to support the replenishment and capital increase agreements negotiated by the previous administration. But he made it clear that U.S. policy toward multilateral development banks was now set on a new course, one based on sharp criticism of the operations of the banks and an ideological opposition to centralized direction of development.

In effect, the Reagan administration did what the Carter administration failed to do: it identified strategic program objectives for U.S. participation in the Bank. One outcome was that the United States dropped its previous opposition to the Bank management's proposal for a new kind of policy-based, structural adjustment lending. The administration came to view this new lending as an important way to advance market-oriented reforms. However, because the administration's objectives were stated in highly ideological terms and aimed at reducing U.S. funding for the Bank, the United States was often at odds with the Bank and other members of the board during the 1980s design and implementation of lending policy.

During IDA 7 replenishment talks in 1983, the United States insisted on holding its pledge to an amount less than it contributed to IDA 6. This position, advanced by the Treasury Department, was supported by President Reagan against the recommendations of the Department of State and the National Security Council. Although other countries expressed willingness to discuss a $12 billion to $16 billion replenishment if the United States carried an appropriate share, the Reagan administration indicated that the maximum it would agree to was a $750 million annual payment and a 25 percent share. The result was a total replenishment of only $9 billion, 25 percent lower than the IDA 6 level. One of the Bank's reasons for recommending a large replenishment was to accommodate the entry of its new client, China. A key element of the administration's stance, however, was that India and China should rely more on commercial borrowing.

In 1985 the administration declined to participate in the new IDA Special Facility for Africa. The Bank and other donors had designed the Facility as a temporary mechanism to channel additional resources to African governments that agreed to implement specific policy reforms after the reduction in U.S. funding had resulted in holding down the size of the IDA 7 replenishment. Also in 1985 President Reagan stated in a budget message to Congress that although the administration intended to honor existing commitments to the IDA and other MDB concessional windows, in light of severe fiscal pressures it was "not budgeting at this time for the future replenishments of these particular institutions."[85] But Congress, which after a brief interlude, had returned to a Democratic majority in both chambers, did not concur. It opposed putting a five-year ceiling on IDA refunding. Congress also authorized $225 million for the IDA-related Special Facility for Sub-Saharan Africa, which the administration had opposed. At the time of the IDA 7 negotiations, the administration had explained that Congress would not exceed the funding ceiling. However, congressional staff indicated in interviews with me that legislative support for the Special Africa Facility was mobilized in explicit contradiction to that claim. And even though the administration never requested appropriation of the special Africa funds, Congress stipulated that some $140 million be allocated in subsequent legislation. Then before negotiations for the next IDA replenishment began, James Baker replaced Donald Regan as Treasury secretary, and the administration rediscovered the importance of the World Bank as an instrument in the deepening debt of less developed countries.

THE DEBT CRISIS AND RENEWED INTEREST IN THE BANK. In August 1982 Mexico suspended payment on its international debt. For more than five years analyses had been warning of impending trouble, but they were the minority view and neither the U.S. government nor the World Bank had forecast the extent of the crisis that ensued throughout the developing world.[86] The initial reactions of U.S. officials to the financial crisis in Mexico has been described as a "dialogue of the deaf."[87] After months of deliberation a bridging loan was arranged, followed by longer-term rescheduling negotiations in conjunction with an IMF stabilization loan. With active U.S. support, the IMF pressed commercial banks to keep lending to Mexico and, subsequently, to others. The IMF and the World Bank also increased their own lending by limited amounts.

In 1982 the United States considered the crisis a problem of short-term liquidity that would recede when the prolonged worldwide recession ended. In 1983, as debtor after debtor experienced continuing difficulties, the Reagan administration reluctantly supported a quota increase for the IMF to enable it to play a catalytic role in mobilizing new lending by commercial banks. The objective of the increase was to avoid the collapse of the international banking system and, to that end, to buy time to allow for renewed growth in the debtor countries. But, consistent with its insistence on the short-term nature of the problem confronting the less developed countries, the administration continued until 1987–88 to oppose a general capital increase for the World Bank.

With an easing of the global recession in late 1983 and 1984, the official U.S. view was that recovery from the "liquidity" problem would follow. The administration also maintained that existing resources were adequate and opposed raising a tightly set ceiling on World Bank policy-based lending. Yet, even after rescheduling, most severely indebted developing countries continued to experience difficulties in servicing their debts, and few showed any resumption of growth. By early 1985 most analysts had concluded that the countries required serious policy reforms and access to more financial resources or debt relief than they were getting.

Faced with the deepening financial crisis in the developing countries and mounting criticism of its policy, the United States revised its policy in the fall of 1985. Although it still considered the debt crisis a short-term liquidity problem, the administration conceded that a more concerted effort was required. In a speech at the World Bank-IMF annual meeting Treasury Secretary James Baker called for new money and a greater role for the Bank. By all accounts the Baker initiative was designed hastily and with little consultation with international financial institutions, other creditor governments, or debtor countries. Nonetheless, the plan included a lead role for the World Bank. Its main elements were a $9 billion increase over planned amounts in World Bank and Inter-American Development Bank lending to fifteen heavily indebted countries, a $20 billion net increase in lending by private banks over three years, and further policy reforms by debtor countries. Combined with previously planned financing, the proposed increase was expected to amount to $20 billion in net new lending by the MDBs after repayments of loans coming due. According to Baker, these steps would help debtor countries adjust and grow their way out of debt.

At least three considerations converged in the redesign of the U.S. debt strategy. First, as commercial banks virtually halted new lending, severe recessions in the debtor countries caused a noticeable decrease in U.S. exports. Second, because the limited size and scope of U.S. bilateral aid precluded substantial funding of the heavily indebted countries and because there were strong pressures from Congress not to bail out the banks, the international financial institutions had to play the lead role in helping to renew growth. Finally, the administration had become convinced that the World Bank's new form of structural adjustment lending could be used as a way to respond to the debt crisis and to advance market liberalizing and private sector policy reforms at the same time. Thus for the next four years the United States encouraged multilateral banks to support policy reforms and pushed them to take the lead in providing new monies themselves and in coordinating the activities of commercial banks. Nonetheless, the Baker plan foundered, as many predicted it would, because of inadequate financing. The private banks failed to provide the full amount of their targeted lending and official capital flows decreased because of negative net IMF flows and decreases in bilateral (mainly export credit agency) flows that were not offset by increased MDB lending.[88]

In mid-December 1988, President-elect George Bush called for a reassessment of the prevailing U.S. international debt strategy. And in March 1989, at the start of the Bush administration, Treasury Secretary Nicholas Brady proposed a successor debt plan that introduced the element of voluntary debt reduction. In offering this proposal the administration adopted what had by then become the prevailing view. The case for debt reduction had been building in academic and other analytic circles for several years.[89] It was being promoted by members of Congress who argued that the United States and other developed countries should do more to help relieve the debt burden of developing countries. The Baker plan, some members argued, only provided a way for the World Bank to bail out the commercial banks; it did not do enough to help countries reduce their debt and restore investment and growth.[90] Also, by the time of Brady's speech, debt reduction was being publicly espoused by some in the banking community and by the managing director of the IMF.[91] The major banks had by that time built reserves and taken other steps that had left them in strengthened positions and removed securing the international banking system as a primary concern.

The Brady proposal, like the Baker plan, insisted on policy reform in the indebted countries as a condition of external support, but it also called for two innovations. First, instead of focusing on new lending, it encouraged multilateral institutions to use their funds to support voluntary write-offs of commercial bank debt. The target was 20 percent, or $70 billion, of the $350 billion debt outstanding. The Brady initiative also proposed that the IMF no longer withhold its own lending to countries until commercial banks agreed to reschedule. As Anne Krueger, former research director of the Bank, has observed, "the Brady Plan gave official acceptance—so long denied—to the view that the existence of debt itself might be a barrier to the resumption of growth in heavily indebted countries. In that way it officially sanctioned debt reduction, whereas earlier U.S. policy had vigorously rejected that alternative."[92]

The idea that World Bank resources might be used to support debt reduction measures was discussed with senior Bank management before being announced. In those discussions the Bank agreed to make a statement that welcomed the new ideas on debt strategy and agreed that a broader menu of options, including measures to reduce the stock of debt and service payments, was important support for countries that performed well. The Bank also indicated preliminary support, pending review of the legal feasibility and costs, for a U.S. idea to use Bank funds to help countries cover interest payments. As stated in a letter from a senior Bank official to the U.S. Treasury, "assuming there are no legal impediments, the formulation of us making a loan, beyond our normal country program limits, seems a very attractive way to cover interest payments. . . . *If* we can guarantee interest, we should also be able to lend for it and the loan approach would avoid a lot of balance-sheet and perceptual problems [with which] we have been concerned."[93] But this time the U.S. initiative met with strong opposition among some members of the Bank, particularly the United Kingdom and Germany, who argued that financing debt reduction was not an appropriate use of World Bank resources. Only after intense debate, which limited the measures that the Bank could take, did the executive board approve a program for implementing the Bank's part of the Brady initiative.

In the implementation of both the Baker and the Brady plans, the U.S. Treasury and the Federal Reserve Board (whose concern was the stability of the banking system) were active participants in IMF, World Bank, and commercial bank negotiations with debtor countries. They also urged commercial banks to continue lending in the first half of the 1980s and to accept some debt reduction in the second half. Finally, according to former chairman of the Federal Reserve Paul Volcker, they "directed" the lending of the Bank.[94] Within the Bank this direction at times raised concerns about the viability of the arrangements being put together for individual countries and the possible effect on the Bank's own portfolio. Two Bank documents, worth quoting at length, disagree with the United States over the adequacy of financing packages and the role of the Bank in securing them. The first is a note prepared for President Barber Conable before a luncheon with Treasury Undersecretary David Mulford.

I want to follow up on the comment made to you by David Mulford to the effect that the difference between the Bank's approach to the Brady Initiative and that of the Fund is a matter of "activism" on the part of the Operations Complex. Naturally, I resent the allegation that the Bank is behaving irresponsibly. But more importantly, this comment indicates a lack of understanding on the part of the U.S. Treasury as to the real reasons why the two institutions have taken somewhat different approaches to a common concern.

In the case of the Fund, the Brady Initiative is being implemented by increasing access to Fund resources, with a specific though legally indirect link to debt and debt service reduction. While this may be a somewhat artificial activity for the Fund, the resources being provided are like all other IMF resources, namely additions to the country's reserves, which the country then uses to effect debt reduction. In the case of the Bank, we are making specific loans that are explicitly for the purpose of debt and debt service reduction. Since this is not an activity that normally falls under the specific investment projects clause of the Articles, we have to justify such lending under the exceptional circumstances provisions, hence we have to satisfy ourselves about the materiality of benefits in terms of growth and increased investment.

This has two important implications. First, the Bank more than the Fund has to be concerned with the adequacy of the financing package over the medium term. If the financing is not adequate, growth may not take place and the material benefits for investment will not be realized. The IMF need not be as concerned with medium term effects; if debt reduction is part of a one-year program, the only thing that would prevent the Fund from supporting it (apart from conditionality) is the Fund's own policy objective of tying debt reduction support to the EFF—something that the Board of the Fund can deal with on a case by case basis.

Second, if the financing package negotiated by the country is inadequate, the Fund can insist on a change in the program, including further adjustment on the part of the country. If financing is too tight to permit growth, that alone would not prevent the IMF from supporting the program of debt reduction. But it could prevent the Bank from doing so, again because of the materiality criteria.

In other words, it is significantly more difficult for the Bank to make loans for debt and debt service reduction than it is for the Fund to increase access for this purpose. This is not a matter of management style. It is anchored in the legal differences in the two institutions. For this reason also our approach to the review of progress under the Brady Initiative was different from that of the Fund. In dealing with financing assurances, the Fund was able to throw the problem back onto the country. In our case, we need to stress up-front the importance of adequate financing. This has a tendency to come across as more interventionist than the Fund, but the alternative is either to let ourselves be 'rolled' on lending standards or block transactions that are already negotiated on grounds that they do not meet the materiality test. We do not have the alternative of simply lending for debt reduction operations as though they were isolated investment projects, detached from the overall medium term adjustment program and financing plan.

. . . This is a matter both of the Articles and of credit risk management, not "activism." It is ironic that the Treasury perceives the Fund to be more supportive of the Brady Initiative than is the

Bank. A close look would show that the Fund management is actually more reserved about the program and—if asked —probably grateful that they do not need to . . . expend as much management energy defending their support for the Initiative on an ongoing basis.[95]

The second document, which expresses many of the same points of disagreement, is an internal Bank memorandum reporting on a meeting with the U.S. Treasury to discuss papers reviewing the Brady debt strategy. After noting that the "tone of the meeting was informal, friendly and constructive," the memorandum went on to outline points in disagreement between the United States and the Bank on the handling of both official and commercial debt.

> The discussion covered a number of topics but two points seemed to be of particular concern: first, Treasury staff are upset at the lack of prior consultation on "proposals" for official debt; second, they have serious reservations about a more pro-active role for the Bank and the Fund in commercial bank debt negotiations. . . . On commercial bank negotiations, Treasury staff criticized the papers as being unbalanced and failing to give adequate recognition to what had been achieved. They seemed most concerned about the suggestion that the Fund and the Bank would get more directly involved in the negotiations, perhaps imposing restraints on the terms of transactions, seeking to shape the modalities of debt and debt service reduction and/or intervening to get the financing gap closed. [A senior official of the department] reiterated the Treasury's view that the "strengthened debt strategy" involves a change in the gap process, and a need on the part of the official institutions to live with more uncertainty and financing risk. He argued that the previous approach produced a false sense of comfort about financing packages and that the new approach could not be launched without the official institutions adopting a different approach on financing assurances.

> [The Bank and Fund representatives] stressed that the key issue is how to strike the right balance between the old critical mass approach and the completely hands-off acceptance of whatever financing could be raised on a voluntary basis. In our view, the pendulum has swung too far away from a disciplined and preagreed

financing plan based on fair burden sharing of all parties. Instead, the commercial banks take the amount of Bank and Fund financing as a given and expect the two institutions to support whatever package they have negotiated with the countries concerned. We do not regard a hands-off approach as acceptable but acknowledge that the degree of intervention required is a matter of judgment.[96]

In sum, in response to the debt crisis the United States turned—belatedly and reluctantly—to the international financial institutions. Consistent with the tilt toward the Fund and Bank, the United States supported an IMF quota increase in 1983, a $12 billion replenishment for the IDA in 1987, and a doubling of Bank capital in 1988. It did not support the debt strategy with other policy initiatives in such areas as aid and trade.[97] But it displayed an unprecedented assertiveness within the Bank in the implementation of the debt strategy and in regard to other policy matters that arose in the second half of the 1980s and the early 1990s.

A New Assertiveness

In the 1987 IDA 8 negotiations, which were completed relatively quickly, the United States agreed to a replenishment that brought IDA lending back to its 1981–83 level in nominal terms and that increased the U.S. annual payment in current dollars to $958 million while holding its share to 25 percent. At the same time, the United States achieved agreement on four policy changes. Two of them—a larger proportion of the total IDA lending dedicated to policy-based lending and a larger IDA share for Sub-Saharan Africa—met with little disagreement from other donors. More controversial were U.S. demands for reducing the maturity of IDA credits (which the Treasury claimed it sought to help win passage of the IDA bill once it went to Congress) and a limit of 30 percent of annual IDA funding that would be available to India and China combined.

In the fall of 1987 in a reversal of its previous opposition, the Reagan administration agreed to a general capital increase of $74.8 billion, but it delayed making a request to Congress until after IDA 8 was approved. As part of the negotiations the United States agreed to release a portion of its Bank shares to other countries, including Japan, but only after obtaining agreement on a change in the Articles of Agreement of the Bank that protected the U.S. veto power.[98] In presenting its request for the capital increase to Congress, the administration emphasized three points: that the Bank, in having taken on a broader responsibility in the debt crisis, had increased its disbursements by more than 40 percent since 1985 and needed additional capital; that the Bank was acting as an important catalyst for economic reforms; and that under its new president, Barber Conable, it had completed a swift and significant reorganization intended to be responsive to matters of high administrative costs that had been raised by the United States for many years. After a year of wrangling with a coalition of liberal congressmen, who objected to a Bank bailout of commercial banks, and conservative congressmen, who continued to condemn the Bank for shoring up socialist regimes, the administration won solid support for the capital increase. The outcome was in part a vote of confidence for Conable, a former member of Congress, and in greater part the result of a renewed executive branch effort to gain support for the Bank.

Three years later in the IDA 9 replenishment talks, the United States again agreed to maintain lending levels in real terms, but it insisted on a ceiling for its own contribution, which led to a further decrease in its share to 21.6 percent. It again demanded the adoption of a number of its policy positions, including continued emphasis on Africa, efforts to improve IDA-IMF collaboration, and greater attention to poverty alleviation as a criterion for IDA allocations, as well as new measures to protect the environment. In contrast to the general policy demands the United States had made in previous replenishment talks, its environmental demands included specific policy and operational reforms: environmental impact assessments of proposed projects, environmental action plans for borrower countries, and disclosure of assessments and plans to local nongovernmental organizations and other concerned groups in advance of loan approvals by the Bank board.[99]

The demands were devised, developed, and successfully advanced in a skillful campaign by nongovernmental organizations. They worked through Congress to force the administration to take up environmental protection and allied themselves with like-minded groups in other countries to build an international consensus on the greening of the World Bank. In early 1983, environmentalists in the United States had begun actively to investigate the environmental impact of Bank project lending and persuaded the House Subcommittee on International Development Institutions and Finance to hold the first oversight hearings on the MDBs and the environment. As one of the leading environmental activists commented in recounting the development of the green campaign against the Bank, witnesses at the hearing described "case after case of environmental and social disasters financed by the Bank, and its sister institutions: huge dams that displaced indigenous peoples, botched irrigation schemes that contributed to the spread of waterborne diseases such as malaria and schistosomiasis . . . cattle ranching schemes that destroyed tropical forests, and massive resettlement projects." Representatives of indigenous peoples' human rights organizations testified on the harm being done to tribal peoples by such projects as the Polonoroeste loan in the Amazon of Brazil.

Several months later the U.S. Treasury forwarded the rebuttals of the MDBs to the House Subcommittee on International Development Institutions and Finance—more than 1,000 pages—that the environmental groups called "evasive and misleading."[100] Following a review of the MDBs' responses, the subcommittee, in consultation with nongovernmental organizations, issued recommendations for reform of the World Bank's environmental protection procedures, many of which Congress passed into law (P.L. 99-190) in late 1985. The law called on the Treasury Department "to monitor environmental aspects of Bank activities, to facilitate constructive U.S. involvement in assuring that sound environmental policies are implemented by multilateral agencies supported by the U.S., and to expedite the flow of information between the Banks and the U.S. Congress, other relevant federal agencies and the public regarding environmental considerations."[101] But the environmental campaign of the nongovernmental organizations did not end there.

In 1984, U.S. environmental activists working together with groups in Brazil developed an extensive research dossier on the Bank's by-then controversial Polonoroeste project, which became the basis of further congressional hearings. A letter was signed by leading individuals and groups that urged the Bank to cease disbursements for Polonoroeste and take steps to improve the ecological design and review of its projects. Dossier and letter were then sent by a representative of Congress to the Bank. A month later the Bank sent a brief response, indicating that Polonoroeste was a carefully planned regional development program and that the Bank would continue to monitor the situation closely and consider concerns raised as the project continued. Senator Robert Kasten of Wisconsin, to whom the environmentalists next turned, sent a letter to

Bank President A.W. Clausen, describing the response as a "brush off" and an "insult," and another letter to Secretary of the Treasury Donald Regan, calling it "outrageous." In March 1985, Clausen aides told Kasten that the environmentalists would get a credible response in a meeting with Clausen and senior management of the Bank. In that meeting, held on May 22, 1985, the Bank acknowledged what had been known for two months—that it had decided to halt funding for Polonoroeste to prevent environmental damage. The Polonoroeste campaign became, in a real sense, the beginning of effective action by like-minded groups around the world. They used modern communications technology to inform one another of crises and to mount in a matter of hours international letter writing and lobbying campaigns to protest other objectionable projects.

In June 1986 the United States cast its first vote against a Bank loan out of concern for the environment. By late 1986 several other countries, including Germany, Sweden, the Netherlands, and Australia, were instructing their executive directors to demand environmental reforms that echoed those urged by the United States. And in May 1987 Bank President Barber Conable announced a series of organizational and operational reforms. To the environmental action groups, the Conable reforms were a marked improvement over previous practices, but they did not go far enough in ensuring that the Bank would regularly take effects on the environment into account in its project and program lending. Therefore, as a result of continued pressure from nongovernmental organizations, U.S. legislation in 1989 (P.L. 101-240) further enjoined U.S. executive directors to the Bank and the other MDBs to propose procedures "for systematic environmental assessment of development projects for which the respective Bank provides financial assistance, taking into consideration the guidelines and principles for Environmental Impact Assessment promulgated by the United Nations Environment Program."[102] The act further required the multilateral banks to make environmental assessments or comprehensive summaries of the assessments available to affected groups and local nongovernmental organizations.

While nongovernmental organizations working through Congress mobilized U.S. pressure for change in Bank environmental policies and practices, it was the U.S. Treasury that took the initiative and promoted examination of the other major U.S. policy issue involving the World Bank: the role of the Bank in the development of the private sector. In marked contrast to the NGO environmental campaign, the promotion of this issue by the Treasury Department involved far less effort to seek international consensus on changes to be sought in Bank policies and less analysis of the challenges and implications for the Bank. The 1981 Treasury assessment of the multilateral development banks had clearly signaled the Reagan administration's intention to move MDB lending policy away from support for state-led growth and toward direct support for development by private enterprise. This effort continued under the Bush administration. But frustrated by its ability to instigate marked change in Bank support for private sector development, the administration brought the issue to a head in the 1990–91 negotiations for an International Finance Corporation capital increase.

Initially, the United States, along with Japan, opposed an IFC capital increase. But when the Japanese government dropped its opposition, the United States, as a condition for its support of the increase, sought to extract concessions on policies it had been promoting for several years. In particular, it sought to tie reforms in the Bank to the IFC negotiations. What it proposed were internal reforms intended to strengthen the Bank's capacity to aid private sector development, a study to explore changes in the Articles of Agreement to remove the prohibition against direct lending to private enterprises (a provision the United States had demanded when the Articles were written), and agreement on a target of 50 percent of total Bank lending in support of the private sector by 1995.

Although other donor countries agreed with the United States that help in developing a country's private sector had become a central challenge for the Bank in light of marked change in development strategies throughout the developing world and the collapse of communism throughout the crumbling Soviet empire, they resented the manner and rejected the content of the U.S. demands. They opposed the demand for a change in the charter and the related lending target. As a fallback position, the United States pressed to get a commitment for a study of Charter reform and for organizational changes within the Bank, but it continued to withhold support for the IFC capital increase while these points were being debated.

In the meantime, in late May 1991 the Foreign Operations Subcommittee of the House Appropriations Committee recommended in a funding bill the $40.3 million U.S. share of the negotiated capital increase, in spite of the fact that the Treasury had not asked for the IFC funds. The subcommittee also chastised the Treasury Department for failure to consult with Congress on its agenda for change in the Bank. The subcommittee report registered regret that the IFC negotiations were being used as a lever to change the Bank and disagreed with the administration's proposals for change. In addition, the subcommittee made its approval of $100 million for the Enterprise for the Americas Initiative (a high priority of the Bush administration) conditional on U.S. support for the IFC.

Several weeks later, at a board meeting scheduled to address the IFC capital increase, the U.S. executive director announced that the United States was prepared to support the increase and called for discussion of papers prepared by the U.S. Treasury on changes proposed in the IFC and the Bank. The board expressed strong opposition to many of the points. The U.S. executive director, on instructions from Treasury official David Mulford, said that under the circumstances the United States would withdraw its support. The meeting was then adjourned on a technicality, the issue was left unresolved, and a week later the United States reversed its position again and agreed to the IFC capital increase, leaving a bitter taste in the mouths of all involved. Overall, the U.S. lack of analytic rigor and highhanded manner hindered its effectiveness in advancing what was, in fact, a timely and important issue for the Bank. Many serious questions about how the World Bank responds to the fundamental changes in the development strategies being pursued by both its long-standing and its new borrowers were glossed over by the U.S. demarche and remain to be answered.

Ironically, the Reagan and Bush administrations, which had wanted to cut back on U.S. participation in the World Bank and other international financial institutions, wound up relying heavily on those institutions to handle problems that the United States could not (for budgetary and other reasons) manage bilaterally. They also pressured the Bank to expand its role in debt relief, macroeconomic policy reforms, environmental protection, private sector development, and the transformation of eastern Europe and the former Soviet Union. Similar U.S. pressure has had great influence on the evolution of Bank activities during its fifty-year history. However, the United States can now no longer exercise the kind of unilateral influence over Bank policies and practices that it once did. There has been a waning of U.S. power in the Bank, due only in part to its steadily declining share of both Bank and IDA funding, and a corresponding change in the way it has sought to exercise its influence in recent years.

Influence on the Bank

Over the years there have been two conflicting opinions of U.S. influence on the Bank. One, held by many members of Congress, argues that the United States has too little influence on what the Bank does. The Bank, it continues, is run by highly paid, aloof bureaucrats, unresponsive to U.S. concerns and accountable only to themselves. The opposite opinion, held by considerable numbers of the Bank staff, nongovernmental groups in borrower countries, and other member countries, maintains that the Bank is run by and under the thumb of the United States. Analysis of the record supports neither position. U.S. influence on the Bank has been important but not absolute.

From the outset the United States considered the Bank an instrument of U.S. foreign policy and used its influence to try to ensure that Bank practices promoted development in ways that complemented U.S. long-term goals and short-term political and economic interests. Although the United States is not the only donor country to use its influence to pursue national interests, the wide scope, frequency, and intensity of its pressure distinguishes it from other donor countries. Its position on specific issues has not always prevailed, but where it has defined an issue as a matter of priority, it has usually had its way. Still, various factors limit the exercise of U.S. influence: the importance to financial markets of nonpoliticized lending decisions; the centrality of burden sharing as a U.S. policy goal; the foreign policy advantage for a donor country to be insulated from tough loan decisions, a protection lost if it is seen as dominating decisions; the clear understanding of all World Bank presidents that the role of the institution depends on its being independent and being seen as independent; and more prevalent opposing views of other donor countries.

The Sources and Strength of U.S. Influence

The basis of U.S. influence derives, on the most fundamental level, from the origins of the Bank and the fact that its Charter and guiding principles have a distinctly American cast. Over the years the United States has used its influence to ensure that those principles are not disregarded.

Table 3. U.S. Contributions and Voting Shares, World Bank and International Development Association, Selected Years, 1946-90[a]

Millions of U.S. dollars unless otherwise specified

Contributions and shares	1946	1950	1960	1970	1980	1990
World Bank						
Subscription	3,175.0	3,175.0	6,350.0	6,350.0	9,347.9	19,606.0
Paid in	158.8	635.0	635.0	635.0	934.8	1,627.6
Percent of total	41.4	38.0	32.9	27.4	23.4	15.7
Voting share (percent)	. . .	34.1	30.3	24.5	21.1	15.1
IDA[b]						
Contribution[c]	. . .	. . .	320.3[d]	1,112.3[e]	6,405.6[f]	14,764.9[g]
Percent of total	. . .	. . .	35.4	31.6	32.9	27.0
Voting share (percent)	. . .	. . .	31.3	25.3	21.5	17.2

Source: World Bank annual reports.

a. For World Bank, expressed in U.S. dollars as of July 1, 1944; for IDA, expressed in U.S. dollars as of January 1, 1960.

b. IDA was established in 1960.

c. Cumulative subscriptions and supplementary resources.

d. Figures are as of June 30, 1961, the date of publication of its first annual report.

e. Expressed in U.S. dollars as of January 1, 1960. Cumulative contribution through IDA 2.

f. Cumulative contribution through IDA 5.

g. Cumulative contribution through IDA 8.

Other sources of U.S. influence include its position as the largest shareholder in the Bank, the importance of its financial market as a source of capital for the Bank (and in the early days the only source), its hold on the position of Bank president and other senior management positions, and the close attention the United States has paid to Bank activities, reinforced by the Bank's location in Washington, D.C. Although its relative importance in many of these dimensions has declined, the United States remains the dominant member of the Bank, in large part because no other country or group of countries has chosen to challenge it.

THE U.S. POSITION AS LEAD SHAREHOLDER. The United States has always had dominant influence on the Executive Board and management of the Bank by virtue of being the largest shareholder and largest contributor to IDA. This is a position it maintains, although the relative size of its Bank shareholding, its share of IDA replenishments, and its corresponding share of votes have decreased (table 3). As a result, Bank management may listen to the views of other donor countries more than it once did, but as in any corporation, it cannot afford to run afoul of its largest shareholder.

The United States is also the dominant member on the Bank's board—but only in part because it is lead shareholder. Formally, most Bank decisions, including those affecting lending levels and loan allocations, require a simple majority vote of the board. This means that the United States, as a major but not majority shareholder, can be outvoted and must marshall support for its views to be decisive. Decisions are, however, often worked out between the United States and Bank management before they ever get to the board, or among members of the board before they get to a vote. And most board decisions are taken by consensus. It is the weight of its voice, therefore, more than the exercise of its vote that gives the United States effective power on the board. And the weight of its voice has been determined by its influence over other major donor countries, especially Germany and Japan.

THE IMPORTANCE OF THE U.S. CAPITAL MARKET. As table 1 showed, U.S. capital no longer plays so dominant a role in total borrowing as it did in the Bank's early years. With the globalization of capital markets and the diversification of the Bank's portfolio, the importance of the U.S. market and U.S. dollar have fluctuated relative to those of other countries. Nonetheless, the United States still accounted for 20 percent of Bank medium- and long-term borrowing by country (before swaps) between 1980 and 1990.

The requirement that the Bank obtain the permission of any country to borrow in its currency has meant that the United States could influence its policies and practices by threatening to deny it access to the U.S. market. That possibility was one of the reasons why Robert McNamara moved quickly after becoming Bank president to diversify the Bank's portfolio and dilute its dollar dependence. The United States has, however, not often denied the Bank access to its market.[103] Even less frequently has it used this authority to put pressure on the Bank. In one instance in the mid-1970s, the United States postponed granting permission to borrow as a means of signaling its displeasure over the Bank's rate of growth. And in 1984 a Treasury official told the Bank's vice president, Ernest Stern, that since it had consistently ignored U.S. concerns about lending to the energy sector, the United States was "reviewing whether the Bank should continue to have access to the U.S. capital markets."[104] In the end, accommodation on energy sector lending was reached and the seriousness of the threat never tested.

For the most part, the imperatives of U.S. monetary policy, not concerns about Bank activities, have been behind the occasional denials or postponements. In the early 1980s, for example, the Reagan administration denied permission to borrow because it said that it wanted to avoid pressure on interest rates. Apparently, it also meant this action to send other members of the Group of Seven advanced industrialized nations a message. The other G-7 countries were concerned that the United States was not managing its fiscal and monetary affairs effectively. The United States told the Bank to raise the funds it sought elsewhere and maintained that this would show the other G-7 countries just how committed it was to prudent economic policy. At the same time, however, the Reagan administration took the lead in getting member countries to agree to liberalize consent procedures for Bank borrowing. The authority to grant or deny access to its market has been, in other words, more an implied than an applied source of power.

Far more significant a source of influence is that were the United States to express serious disinterest in the Bank or serious concern over its financial state of affairs, the effect on the financial markets would likely be immediate.[105] It is this perhaps more than anything else that makes the Bank take particular note of U.S. views. This influence has gradually been tempered by the Bank's leverage over the United States as a result of the large stake that U.S. bondholders have come to have in it and the size of the claim on U.S. callable capital that could be made should Bank lending run into serious trouble. These mitigate interference on political grounds in either the Bank's borrowing or lending operations.

THE U.S. HOLD ON THE BANK PRESIDENCY AND STAFF. By tradition rather than formal rule, the United States has the prerogative to name the president of the World Bank. It has always nominated a U.S. citizen. This prerogative was initially granted not only because the United States was the Bank's largest shareholder but also because it was the key guarantor and principal capital market for Bank bonds. The market's view was important, for example, in the appointment of John McCloy instead of Graham Towers of Canada. But as U.S. support for the Bank has waned and the relative importance of the U.S. market has declined, this privilege has been called into question. Had the United States not nominated McNamara to a second term, it is likely that other countries would have usurped the privilege. And when it came time to select his successors, concern that conservative influences in the Reagan and Bush administrations would put forward candidates unacceptable to the international community led to talk of finding non-American alternatives. For example, having decided to resign, Barber Conable worried that Treasury Secretary Nicholas Brady had no serious interest in the appointment of his successor and therefore appealed directly to President Bush. Noting that there was a lot of dissatisfaction with U.S. leadership in the Bank, Conable warned the president that unless he nominated a person of stature, the Europeans and Japanese would take the privilege away from the United States.[106] In each instance, however, an acceptable U.S. candidate was identified and the American prerogative sustained.

The history of the World Bank shows that the choice has been critical to the life of the institution, although the impact of the person selected has not always been foreseeable. The United States has a record of nominating people who have Wall Street or Washington, not development, experience but who end up fervently championing both the institution and the need to tackle global poverty. This was as true of George Woods as of Robert McNamara, whose appointment reflected more a way for McNamara to escape the stigma of U.S. Vietnam War policy than a commitment on President Johnson's part to strong Bank leadership. Not surprisingly, there was much international consternation over the appointment. Each Bank president has also asserted independence from the United States. Even Conable, who of all the recent presidents was criticized for being too much under the thumb of the U.S. government, sought in the later years of his term to assert the Bank's independence. In 1990, for example, he pushed the executive board to support renewed lending to China despite congressional and administration opposition. Nonetheless, the privilege of selecting the Bank's president has ensured, at a minimum, a general policy orientation compatible with that of the United States.

The high proportion of Americans on the Bank staff has also been said to provide the United States with reinforcing influence. This claim has become moot as the proportion of U.S. nationals on the professional staff has contracted from 60 percent in 1951 to 26 percent in 1991.[107] Nonetheless, the United States has regularly urged that U.S. citizens be put in key management positions. For a time, it insisted on having U.S. directors in charge of the Latin American, Central American, and Caribbean regions (though this has not been true since the mid-1970s). And in many years Americans have held one or more vice presidential positions. Perhaps more significant, many staff members have been trained in the United States. But the U.S. economics profession is not itself of one mind, so the nature of the selection from within the profession is what seems to reinforce and sustain an institutional mind-set. Many on the outside view this in-breeding as extending not only to those brought onto the staff but also to the circle of consultants used to referee or participate in research efforts.

U.S. ATTENTION TO THE BANK. The United States has paid closer attention to the Bank than has any other major shareholder and has frequently flexed its muscle. As a result, even with its relative loss of power in the Bank, the United States still dominates largely by default. Neither Japan nor the western European nations as a group have yet shown sufficient interest to challenge U.S. leadership.

The United States is the only country that carries out detailed reviews of every Bank loan proposal and the only one to maintain constant contact with the Bank through government officials in addition to its representative to the board. Often, the United States will question a prospective loan early in the preparation process. And during final deliberation of a loan proposal by the Bank's executive board, it will make comments designed to draw attention to general matters of concern in order to influence future lending. Bank policy papers, evaluation reports, and special studies are also closely monitored. Executive branch officials have often emphasized that these procedures provide the United States with a substantial measure of influence and have repeatedly offered examples to illustrate the extent to which the Bank has been willing to make changes in loan and policy proposals on U.S. recommendations.[108]

Formal responsibility for conveying U.S. views and carrying out U.S. policy in the Bank rests with the U.S. executive director, who with other directors has the authority (under Article V, sections 1 and 2) over all Bank decisions. Far more important than the executive director, however, is the direct and constant interaction between the Bank and the U.S. Treasury. This interaction occurs daily at the staff level in regard to the detailed reviews of loan proposals and other routine matters. It occurs frequently at higher levels at the initiative of both the Bank and the U.S. government, especially, but not only, in regard to countries of importance to the United States.

The intensity of Bank-Treasury interaction is a unique feature of U.S. relations with the Bank, obviously facilitated by the Bank's location in Washington. As Bank files indicate, the U.S. government has privileged access to it that differs significantly from that of other member countries. The United States is sometimes consulted on a matter before other members are. It has regularly received early drafts of papers and studies, (they are now also circulated to other members in draft). And the top management of the Bank spends much more time meeting with, consulting, and responding to the United States than it does any other member country.

Although this intense interaction has changed little over the years, the way the United States mobilizes other member countries in support of its views has changed considerably. Initially, it was so predominant that its positions and the decisions of the board were virtually indistinguishable. For the most part, other member countries simply followed its lead, not only because of the strength of its support of the Bank but also because of the quality of its leadership.[109] But as the strength and quality declined, the United States could not count on automatic support. It began, therefore, to go outside the board with increasing frequency. Since the late 1970s it has made demarches to G-7 counterparts in national capitals as well as to executives on the Bank board. Building a working relationship with G-7 counterparts in capitals was a deliberate strategy of the Carter administration and was largely aimed at counteracting the mounting opposition to the Bank in Congress. Although this strategy broke down during the Reagan retrenchment, the Treasury returned to it in the second half of the 1980s in an effort to mobilize support for policy initiatives on debt in less developed countries, on China, and on the environment.

The Treasury has exerted decisive pressure by threatening to withhold its support from replenishment and capital increase negotiations. Although in earlier years the aim was to pressure others to a larger share of IDA funding, the tactic came to be used for other purposes. In the late 1970s, in response to repeated congressional delays in the passage of IDA funding bills, the United States and the other donor countries developed procedures or triggers that defined the level of commitment required for replenishment to go into effect. These triggers were set at a level of 85 percent of IDA voting stock so as to require U.S. participation. While the intention of the triggers was to hold U.S. feet to the fire, they gave the United States a de facto veto over IDA refunding because a threat to withhold its contribution could put not just the U.S. share but an entire replenishment negotiation in jeopardy. And this is a power the United States has come to use to assert its views on major issues of policy. That is, it has made major decisions on policy issues conditions of its participation in IDA replenishments and Bank and IFC capital increases. In this way it has furthered positions for which it may not have had majority support on the executive board.

The Exercise of U.S. Influence

Over the years the United States has used multiple sources of influence pervasively, episodically, and often inconsistently in pursuit of both long-term foreign policy goals and short-term political and economic interests. In so doing it has been driven by contradictory but simultaneously held attitudes toward the Bank. On the one hand it has looked to the Bank to promote development and an open world economy. On the other hand it has considered the Bank but one of its many instruments of foreign policy—a source of funds to be offered or denied to reward friends, punish enemies, or advance any number of other objectives defined by domestic constituency groups or immediate foreign policy aims.

To a considerable extent the United States has used its influence in ways that have strengthened and supported the dominant mission of the Bank. One of the major longer-term U.S. aims has been to increase the resources available for reconstruction and development while containing the burden on its own budget of providing that financing. In this effort it has been more than moderately successful. As its annual reports show, total Bank lending increased from $250 million in 1947 to $21 billion in 1992 (including IDA but not IFC loans), but the U.S. share of the amount shrank significantly. Thus a dollar of U.S. budgetary outlays leverages considerably more development resources now than it did at the start-up of the Bank. A second U.S. objective has been to develop the Bank's capacity to promote development—in ways consistent with U.S. political and economic interests. The United States has brought considerable influence to bear on matters of broad policy, specific country and sector lending decisions, and Bank administration and management.

DEVELOPMENT POLICY. The United States generally endorsed expanding both the geographic and substantive scope of the Bank's lending program. This support has not precluded it from using its influence at times to block or water down proposals to change Bank policies and practices. For example, during the drafting of the Bank's Charter, the United States argued against allowing direct lending to private enterprises. It resisted proposals for substantial increases in program lending in the 1950s and 1960s and fought proposals to increase local currency costs of projects. In the late 1970s it opposed the idea of structural adjustment lending proposed by the Bank's management. Among the reasons given were that the initiative contravened the Articles of Agreement of the Bank and that limited program lending had already been tried and had failed. It took Bank management three years to sell structural adjustment lending to the United States and other skeptical member countries. Not until confronted with the debt crisis and the need to find a way to avoid a collapse of the international financial system did the United States revise its position.

For the most part, however, on the broad issues of development policy and strategies, U.S. and World Bank views have evolved together, at least until disputes in the 1980s over specific policy issues, notably the increased support of private enterprise. Major changes in Bank development policy, especially changes in the sector allocation of Bank lending, were actively if at times belatedly supported by the United States. In the 1950s and early 1960s the United States initiated and encouraged major changes in development assistance policy, especially the increased focus on agricultural production. The Bank followed the U.S. lead and worked in concert with the U.S. bilateral aid program in the field. This interaction was particularly intense when the United States was providing large amounts of aid to India and in Latin America at the time of the Alliance for Progress. In the 1970s the McNamara Bank and the United States shifted simultaneously toward more poverty-oriented development policies. Thus the United States supported the Bank's reorientation from infrastructure projects to agriculture and rural development and later to education, health care, and population control projects. These changes were advocated by members of the development profession in the United States, viewed as shared goals of member countries, and considered generally noncontentious.[110] But in the 1980s this close coincidence of views broke apart.

The United States, the Bank, and most member countries came to broad agreement on the importance of crucial economic policy reforms to be advanced through Bank lending for structural adjustment. Indeed, this approach was labeled "the Washington consensus" in recognition of the convergence of views on reforms advocated by Washington-based institutions, the Bank, and the IMF. But beyond agreement on a core of reforms needed to bring about macroeconomic equilibrium, the consensus did not hold. And the United States, whose positions on some issues conveyed a strong ideological orientation favoring the private sector, was often sharply at odds with both Bank management and other member countries.

For instance, the United States expressed concern that the Bank was not serving, as it should have, as a lender of last resort. In opposition to the Bank's view that adjustment often required substantial financing, the U.S. pushed for reductions in lending levels while urging the Bank to increase pressure on countries to reform. Disputes between the United States and the Bank on this matter emerged in regard to lending to countries such as India that the United States believed ought to be relying more on private finance, lending for oil and gas exploration, and more generally in discussions about replenishments and capital increases for IDA and the Bank. Also, although the United States and the Bank agreed on the need to promote market-based reforms, they differed on the importance to be attached to private ownership and, more generally, the role of the state in the economy. This difference was particularly marked in the U.S. response to Bank lending in the energy sector. Although neither the Bank management nor other member countries agreed, the United States sought to prohibit loans to national oil companies.

The handling of the debt crisis was another major policy matter on which U.S. and Bank views diverged. Through most of the 1980s the Bank followed the U.S. lead on handling the crisis and did not venture proposals for new actions. Before the announcement of the Brady proposal, the Bank was widely criticized for not taking more initiative and for being reluctant to cross the U.S. Treasury. In early 1988, for example, commercial bank lenders to Brazil tried to get the Bank to insure a portion of a new loan package under negotiation, but the Treasury opposed the idea on the grounds that it was unnecessary and might foster the impression that such guarantees should be common.[111] Later in the spring, Conable sent to the board a Bank debt study suggesting the need for an expanded Bank role in facilitating new money packages and other forms of financial relief, including debt-reduction schemes. The report also noted that consensual debt relief, including outright forgiveness, might be the only workable solution for some debtors. In its annual world debt report released early the following year, the Bank noted again that the debtor countries' position had stubbornly failed to improve and that "imagination and resolve" were needed. But absent from this public document were any recommendations of its own. Only after the Brady proposals were made did the Bank publicly endorse debt reduction and an expanded Bank function. In implementing the Brady initiative, however, the Bank was at times at odds with the United States, especially on the size of the financial packages that needed to be put together for some countries.

The most visible dispute, however, was over the U.S. effort to tie the 1991 IFC capital increase to major reforms in the Bank's private sector development activities. In a sense this marked the culmination of a decade-long effort to force the Bank to take direct actions to promote development of the private sector in borrowing countries. Although other member countries—both developed and developing—generally concurred that the Bank needed to support private sector development more strongly, they did not accept the ideological tenor of the U.S. pressure nor many of the specific reform notions the U.S. sought to impose. In 1992 the Japanese government requested that the Bank review the Asian development experience, which represented an alternative market-based development approach distinct from the U.S. model and prescriptions.

COUNTRY AND SECTOR ALLOCATIONS. The country and sector allocations of Bank lending have also experienced U.S. influence, though less heavily than is often assumed. Bank lending and U.S. policy interests have usually converged, and the United States has not often interfered directly in specific loan decisions. Along with other donor countries, it has accepted Bank lending to countries with which it was not on good terms. And, more often than not, it has accepted the sectoral composition of Bank lending in individual countries. But the United States has repeatedly used its influence, directly and controversially, to affect decisions relating to both particular countries and certain commodity areas. The record is mixed on the actual impact of this pressure. In many cases the Bank resisted the interference. In the early 1970s, for example, it made loans to India and Egypt despite U.S. objections; in the midst of the Vietnam War, it resisted U.S. pressure to lend to South Vietnam; and despite congressional opposition, the Bank has made loans to various developing countries to expand production of palm oil and other commodities competitive with U.S. products. Yet a heavy U.S. hand has been laid on some loan decisions, and although instances of strong U.S. interference do not account for the direction of most Bank lending, they have been a source of tension between the United States and both the Bank management and Bank board.

In the main, the United States has been willing to have money put where it is most needed or could be used most effectively. And it has been willing to vote against a loan to a friendly country on economic or technical grounds, sometimes to the dismay of the State Department. Nonetheless, like some other donor countries, the United States has regularly encouraged the Bank to lend to favored countries. As a former Bank official said in 1970, "the French are always pressing us to slant IDA funds toward French Africa. Similarly, the Japanese, whose interest is in Southeast Asia, are persuading us to put more assistance into that area. And the United States, I need scarcely add, is always telling us that more funds should be channeled into Latin America."[112]

More than other donor countries, the United States has also tried to block loans to "problem" countries. In those instances in which lending has been reduced or denied, the Bank has always had reasoned economic arguments for its decision. Strictly speaking, therefore, it has often concurred with rather than conceded to U.S. pressures. But throughout the Bank's history there have been particular cases of strong pressure from high-level U.S. officials either to lend or not to lend to specific countries.

This pressure has been in evidence since the Bank's earliest days. In 1947, for example, John McCloy, with the encouragement of the U.S. Department of State, decided that the Bank's first loan would go to France. The Communist party had won a minor position in the coalition government, and the U.S. government feared that it might increase its mandate in the next election. The loan carried tough terms, which the French government protested but accepted. The Bank would lend only half of the $500 million the French requested, and it would closely supervise the French economy to ensure that the government took steps to balance its budget, increase taxes, and cut consumption of certain luxury imports. In addition, the State Department "informed the French that they would have to 'correct the present situation' by removing any communist representatives in the Cabinet. The Communist party was pushed out of the coalition government in early May 1947, and within hours, as if to underscore the linkage, McCloy announced that the loan would go through."[113]

Also in the spring of 1947 the Bank entered into negotiations with Poland for a $128.5 million loan for coal-mining equipment—much scaled down from Poland's request for $600 million. The *New York Times* reported that although the Polish loan was considered a sound investment, the United States objected, fearing "the political effect of such a credit to Poland's Communist-led government."[114] Nonetheless, the Bank sent a team to Poland in mid-1947 to evaluate the project. The resulting favorable staff report was followed in the fall by a visit to Poland by Bank President McCloy and the subsequent start of formal negotiations of a loan for some $50 million. But the Department of State made clear that it would oppose even a small loan, and McCloy "privately made it known" to interested Bank members "that he now thought his Wall Street investors would not approve."

> Instead, in their negotiations with the Poles, McCloy and Garner now began to raise conditions that they knew to be unacceptable. They demanded that Poland first stabilize its currency according to guidelines issued by the International Monetary Fund. Instead of $45 million, the Bank's loan committee suggested $25 million, and even that was to be contingent on the Poles' agreeing to sell their coal to Western Europe and use the hard-currency proceeds to make payments on the Bank's loan. Poland's executive director at the Bank and its ambassador in Washington—both anticommunists—tried to persuade their government to accept these unusually tough terms. But, since they had originally sought $600 million, the $25 million the Bank offered now was hardly incentive enough for the Polish Communists to agree to such concessions also. Simultaneously, a firm consensus developed within the Truman administration rejecting the notion that Western aid might help preserve the coalition government in Warsaw. . . . So, finally, in mid-1948, Eugene Black told McCloy that he had been formally instructed by the Truman administration to vote against any loan for Poland. McCloy then suspended all further negotiations with the Poles.[115]

The rejection of a loan to Czechoslovakia at roughly this same time underscored the U.S. position against World Bank lending to Eastern Europe. In both the Czech and Polish cases the World Bank justified its refusal on the grounds that political uncertainty undermined each country's status as a good credit risk. As stated in the Bank's 1948 *Annual Report*,

> the Bank is not unmindful of the importance of the economic development of its member countries in Europe which are not participants in the ERP.

It is unfortunate but nonetheless true that the existing political difficulties and uncertainties in Europe present special problems which have thus far prevented the Bank from making loans in those countries. The Bank is fully cognizant of the injunction in its Articles of Agreement that its decisions shall be based only on economic considerations. Political tensions and uncertainties in or among its member countries, however, have a direct effect on economic and financial conditions in those countries and upon their credit position.[116]

The political situation did not change in ways that opened prospects for Bank lending, and Poland and Czechoslovakia withdrew from Bank membership in the 1950s.

There are additional examples in each decade of decisions not to lend following strong U.S. pressure. For the most part the cold war provided the reason through the end of the 1980s. The effort in the 1950s to negotiate financing for the construction of the Aswan Dam in Egypt provides an illustration.[117] In July 1956 the withdrawals of American and then British offers to join the Bank in financing the dam were followed within a week by President Gamal Abdal Nasser's decision to nationalize the properties of the foreign-owned Suez Canal Company. In response, France, Britain, and Israel initiated military action against Egypt.

The Bank's relation to the Aswan Dam project had been a long and complicated one. Suffice it to say here that despite the staff's support for the project, which would have carried with it stiff conditions agreed to after difficult negotiations with Egypt, the United States and Britain were deterred from joint financing largely by Nasser's expression of Arab nationalism and support for discontented elements in several Arab countries. As Bank negotiations were nearing closure, support in the U.S. Department of State for a resolution of the affair began to diminish, in part in response to growing congressional opposition. "In March 1956, when the foreign aid bill for the fiscal year 1957 was presented to a House Subcommittee on Appropriations, no congressman defended the Aswan Dam financing against attack."[118] In mid-May, Nasser gave diplomatic recognition to Communist China, which further dissipated State Department support. Although Bank president Eugene Black and the Egyptian ambassador in Washington continued to promote the project, Secretary of State John Foster Dulles indicated on July 19, 1956, that the United States had decided not to participate. The following day the

British financing offer was withdrawn. Ultimately, the Bank's offer lapsed, since it no longer had any financial partners.

During the 1960s and into the 1970s the United States sought to block Bank lending in a number of cases involving disputes over the expropriation of U.S. private property, especially in Latin America. Under pressure from the United States, the Bank had developed a formal policy, explained in a 1969 publication:

> The Bank is charged, under its articles of agreement, to encourage international investment. It has, therefore, a direct interest in the creation and maintenance of satisfactory relations between member countries and their external creditors. Accordingly, the normal practice is to inform governments who are involved in such disputes that the Bank or IDA will not assist them unless and until they make appropriate efforts to reach a fair and equitable settlement.[119]

Thus a settlement need not have been reached as long as "appropriate efforts" to this end were made by a prospective borrower. This left room for interpretation of the facts and disagreement with the United States, which generally urged a strict ruling but did not always get its way. Strong U.S. pressure was followed by reduced Bank lending to Peru after its nationalization of the International Petroleum Company in 1969. In contrast, the Bank made a loan to Guyana in 1971 despite U.S. opposition. Although the U.S. government did not consider that Guyana was doing enough to resolve an expropriation dispute, Bank management and a majority of the Bank board did.

The Bank suspended lending to Chile from 1970 to 1973 following the election of Salvador Allende and his nationalization of the Chilean copper mines. Although the suspension is often cited (even by the U.S. government) as an instance in which U.S. pressure was decisive, the actual record is complex. Indeed, the details provide a particularly interesting picture of the interface between U.S. pressure and World Bank decisionmaking.

The United States pressured the Bank not to lend to the Allende government after nationalization of Chile's copper mines. Despite the pressure, the Bank sent a mission to Santiago (having determined that Chile was in compliance with Bank rules requiring that for lending to resume after a nationalization, procedures for compensation had to be under way). Robert McNamara subsequently met with Allende to indicate

that the Bank was prepared to make new loans contingent upon government commitments to reform the economy. But the Bank and the Allende
regime could not come to terms on the conditions for a loan. Throughout
the period of the Allende regime, Chile received no new loans.[120]

Shortly after Allende's assassination in 1973 during a coup that
brought General Pinochet's military junta to power, the Bank resumed
lending, providing a fifteen-year credit for copper mine development. A
retrospective internal Bank memorandum concluded that the Bank had
made errors of both professional and tactical judgment in this sequence of
decisions. It had failed to support the underlying social objectives of the
Allende regime and therefore did not position itself to make the legitimate
point that the economic costs of the government's program were
unnecessarily high and could be reduced by proper economic management.
Conversely, in lending to the junta the Bank ignored the retreat from long-
term social objectives and the high social costs of the economic reforms.
Moreover, the memorandum argued, the Bank made the mistake of not
bringing the decision to suspend lending to Allende's government to the
executive board so that it would be seen as a board action. Nowhere did
the memorandum refer to pressure from the United States.[121] In an
interview in 1991 McNamara said that U.S. pressure was not the cause of
the Bank's decision to refuse to lend. Rather, he explained, the Bank
simply could not justify lending under the economic conditions that
prevailed.[122] Still, the sequence of decisions on Chile was clearly
consistent with U.S. policy objectives. The suspension of lending in
1970–73 was cited in the 1982 U.S. Treasury report as a significant
example of the successful exercise of U.S. influence on the Bank. And
although the Bank reached an agreement in principle on new lending in
June 1973, the loan proposals were not formally considered by the board
until after the September coup that brought General Pinochet to power. As
a Bank white paper explained, preliminary reactions to the proposals by
several executive directors "raised a serious question as to whether the
proposals would command a favorable vote at that time. Hence, after
consultation with the Government of Chile, the management postponed
indefinitely the placing of this item on the agenda of the Executive
Directors, and this is how matters stood at the time that the Allende
government was deposed."[123]

Ironically, in the later years of the Pinochet regime the U.S. government
asked the Bank to postpone board discussion of a structural adjustment

loan to Chile to avoid congressional opposition on human rights grounds at a time when the administration was seeking support for Bank refunding. But in a letter to James Baker, the assistant secretary of the Treasury, on October 29, 1986, Barber Conable rejected the U.S. request.

The Bank's decision not to lend to Vietnam in the late 1970s was another instance in which strong U.S. pressure was exerted. Although McNamara said at the time and maintained in later interviews that the decision was made by the Bank on economic considerations, at least some of the staff servicing Asian countries felt otherwise. A memo to McNamara and a long "private note" written in August and September of 1979 by a senior Bank official for East Asia and the Pacific region summarize the views of two economic missions to Vietnam.[124] The first mission in 1978 led to the beginnings of project preparation work on a modest scale. The level of funding earmarked for Vietnam was held by McNamara to $150 million, far below the $400 million the allocative norms would have subscribed to the country.

The Bank's mission reported that economic conditions were not favorable, that economic management left much to be desired, but that there was no case for suspending the Bank's meager engagement there. Indeed, Shahid Husain, the head of the mission, reported in a memo to McNamara that it was the judgment of the mission that Vietnam's economic performance could not be rated lower than that of some other IDA borrowers in the region, including Bangladesh and Pakistan, and that experience on project implementation in Vietnam was actually better. Although in the wake of massive refugee flows Vietnam faced serious international criticism and it would therefore be inappropriate to take a project to the board, "there are reasonable prospects that in due course we should be able to build a meaningful dialogue on economic and development issues. So, while being responsive to the environment, we should try to keep our channels open to the Vietnamese."[125] The mission's contention, in contrast to what McNamara said publicly in *Newsweek*, was that on substantive grounds there was no basis for stopping all lending to Vietnam. The Bank should wait until it could get sufficient support for lending from the board. Thus the staff in charge of the region did not support a suspension of lending on economic grounds; but whether McNamara was driven by strong U.S. and other donor pressure or his own determination remains open to debate.

A more recent example in which the Bank's refusal to lend clearly coincided with U.S. policy is that of Nicaragua in the 1980s. The reason for the suspension of lending was the accumulation of arrears. However, in September 1984 the Nicaraguan government formally proposed a solution to its arrearages problem. The proposal encompassed three actions: a freeze until the end of 1984 on disbursements and repayments, preparation and appraisal by the World Bank of an economic adjustment program for presentation to the board before the end of June 1985, and a loan rescheduling or loan repayment in local currency. The third measure, the Nicaraguan government noted, was consistent with Article IV, section 4(c) of the Articles of Agreement, which provides, "if a member suffers from an acute exchange stringency, so that the service of any loan contracted by that member or guaranteed by it or by one of its agencies cannot be provided in the stipulated manner, the member concerned may apply to the Bank for a relaxation of the conditions of payment." In the view of senior Bank staff, such actions would have entailed substantial danger for the Bank's "market image" and "shareholder relations."[126] Its response, which in Nicaragua's view showed "an absence of a constructive attitude on the part of the Bank," was to insist that the country settle its overdue payments in full and negotiate a stabilization program with the IMF.[127] Only when those two conditions were met would the Bank be in a position to help with the preparation of a medium-term program. No concerted effort was made, however, to help the Sandinista regime meet these conditions, as was done, for example, in response to Zambia's arrearage problems later in the 1980s.

Although one need not dispute the Bank's economic policy assessments of Allende's Chile, Vietnam, and Nicaragua under the Sandinistas, it is worth noting that equally harsh assessments could have been made, but were not, of Somoza's Nicaragua, Marcos's Philippines, and Mobutu's Zaire, regimes that were all important cold war allies of the United States.

Instances in which the United States successfully influenced increases or more rapid lending to a particular country are even harder to pin down unequivocally because of the broad concurrence of U.S. geopolitical interests and Bank country allocations. But examples exist in each of the Bank's decades. For instance, the United States influenced increased lending to Japan in the 1950s despite the Bank's reluctance because of the country's inadequate creditworthiness.[128] It is ironic that the United States pushed the Bank to finance steel projects in Japan, given that country's managed approach to industrialization and later U.S. opposition to lending to the steel sector in many other countries.

Two more recent examples of seemingly favorable treatment of countries important to the United States involve Bank decisions to release structural adjustment financing despite assessments by staff that conditions did not warrant lending. In 1988 the Bank provided the first tranche of a sectoral adjustment loan to the government of Argentina despite the fact that an IMF stabilization program had been held up because of differences between the Fund and the government, including differences over the size of the country's deficit.[129] Treasury and World Bank officials have since said that the United States was interested in helping Argentine President Raul Alfonsin and had indicated to the Bank that it would support a decision to release funding to Argentina even in the absence of an IMF program. Despite opposition by some of its staff, the Bank released the funds. The United States, under a change of leadership at the Treasury, then reversed itself and openly criticized the Bank's action.[130]

During the Persian Gulf crisis, Secretary of State James Baker offered Turkey support for increased Bank lending in appreciation for the country's assistance against Iraq. After Baker's visit, the World Bank released the second tranche of a sector adjustment loan that had previously been held up because of Turkey's failure to satisfy the Bank's loan conditions even though the IMF judged the country's macroeconomic performance remained unsatisfactory.[131] According to one study of World Bank policy-based lending, a large number of country cases reveal this same phenomenon—that although alliance with the United States does not earn a recipient country gentler loan conditions, it does yield "a more forgiving treatment of slippage on conditions."[132]

U.S. pressures on the Bank in regard to loans for the production of certain commodities intensified in the 1970s. In the Bank's early days the United States did not want it to lend directly to private companies nor act as a substitute for private lending. In the 1970s pressure was applied, some of it mandated by Congress, in an attempt to prevent Bank support for increasing production of commodities that competed with those of producers in the United States. In most instances of congressionally mandated opposition to commodity loans—for palm oil or citrus products, for example—Bank management stood up to the United States and successfully gained executive board approval. This was the case with a loan for palm oil production to Papua-New Guinea, which the United States tried to block in the late 1970s. But U.S. opposition was not without effect. U.S. legislation and U.S. position in the Bank were cast in terms of opposition to loans for commodities that were in surplus on the world market. The impact of this position was to make the Bank especially careful in its consideration of rates of return in these commodity areas. From the staff's point of view there was quite simply a higher burden of proof for products singled out by the United States.[133]

For certain other commodities, notably steel, mined products, oil, and gas, it was the U.S. administration even more than Congress that strongly opposed Bank lending. The Bank's decision in March 1987 to limit support for steel projects to providing technical assistance, thereby stopping loan requests from India and Pakistan, was the result, at least in part, of strong U.S. opposition over a number of years. In 1985 the United States had voted against an IFC equity investment in a steel project in Brazil and later opposed a Bank steel sector restructuring loan to Mexico (which was approved in 1988). The case of Mexico provides, however, an interesting example of conflicting American objectives and the nuances of U.S. opposition votes. The matter arose at a time when Bank and Mexico debt management and policy reform efforts were beginning to work well. For the Bank to retreat on a project that was well advanced would have seriously undermined the efforts, Besides, the United States had a keen interest in seeing a successful resolution to Mexico's debt crisis. It therefore voted against the loan, but it did not try to change the views of other members of the board, which it knew would support the loan. Congressional requirements were thus satisfied, although all parties were fully aware that the loan approval was never in doubt.

The United States also voted against but did not oppose with much vehemence a steel sector loan to China at a time in the 1980s of warm U.S.-China relations. Yet in other cases where U.S. interests were not strong, opposition to steel sector lending was more forceful and projects were shelved.[134] According to former Bank Vice President Burke Knapp, U.S. opposition to steel production loans in the 1980s had as much to do with opposition to the Bank's lending to large state enterprises as to its lending for steel production per se. The United States had not objected to earlier steel sector loans to Japan, where production was in the hands of private companies, but consistently opposed support for state-owned steel enterprises in developing countries as more and more producers came into the market.

In mining, the United States argued against Bank lending both on grounds of oversupply in the world market and the availability of private finance for worthy investments. For instance, the United States blocked consideration of a request by a Brazilian joint venture mining company for an IFC loan that was intended to boost Brazil's export of iron ore.[135] It also opposed a major IFC investment in the Escondida copper project in Chile. Escondida is one of the world's largest and richest copper ore bodies. U.S. copper producers were clearly concerned about the added competition and the potential for the new mine to drive low world copper prices even lower. However, the IFC estimated the impact of Escondida on copper prices to be "modest and transitory." And both Japan and Germany, which viewed Escondida as a stable long-term source of supply, were expected to provide the bulk of the loan financing in exchange for long-term service contracts. As a result, U.S. objections were not sustained and the investment went ahead.

After the oil price shock of 1973–74 the United States supported increased Bank lending in the energy sector. Much of what the Bank undertook was then noncontroversial. However, lending for oil and gas exploration and development became a matter of serious dispute between the United States and the Bank, especially after the change from the Carter administration to the Reagan administration. In the opinion of Edward Fried, U.S. executive director at the Bank during part of the Carter years, a serious effort should have been made to increase oil production and conserve use in developing countries because they were going to be big users as well as potential sources of supply.[136] The question was what the role of the Bank should be.

From the U.S. point of view, it was a bad idea for the Bank to spend money on oil drilling, but the institution could be influential in promoting exploration and development. Toward the end of the 1970s Sheikh Ahmed Zaki Yamani of Saudi Arabia proposed in a speech that the World Bank and oil surplus economies cooperate to boost energy sector development in the developing world. The idea was picked up by Fried and after discussion with the Bank put forward as a proposal for an energy affiliate that would provide a way of enlarging and concentrating the Bank's work in the whole energy field. The proposal moved ahead until the Reagan administration withdrew U.S. support. The new administration not only considered the affiliate another window for increasing the lending of the Bank, which it opposed, but also argued that financing for oil and gas production should come from the private sector. The World Bank could foster policies that encouraged private sector investment, but it should not make loans to governments or state-owned oil and gas companies.[137] A U.S. note to World Bank directors explaining the new administration's opposition to the energy affiliate said that the United States would not approve development bank action that borrowed from private capital markets to make long-term loans to governments of developing countries for energy development.[138]

Following its defeat of the energy affiliate proposal, the United States continued to oppose the Bank's energy lending policy and specific loan proposals not consistent with an emphasis on private sector financing and investment. A series of internal Bank memos reporting on conversations with the Treasury and the U.S. executive director in April and May 1984 make clear the nature and intensity of the dispute between the United States and the Bank (including both management and members of the board). In the conversations a Treasury official expressed concern over the Bank's "undue enthusiasm" for oil and gas lending that, he stated, could and should have been left to the private sector. Referring in one conversation to a specific Nigerian gas engineering loan as a scandal, he argued that Nigeria was a rich country and could easily secure the financing for itself. In response to the assessment that Nigeria could not get commercial bank financing at that time, he stated, "that was their own fault." They had "messed up" and could in due course restore their creditworthiness. Although a Bank representative made the point that the Bank was not like other lenders because it sought to improve the policy framework, establish appropriate prices, and improve production incentives, the Treasury official emphasized that the United States would continue to oppose loans to national oil companies and loans where it deemed private financing to be attainable.[139]

In subsequent Board discussions and votes the United States insisted that Bank lending not displace private equity and lending. To this end, it proposed two lending guidelines: there should be no Bank oil and gas lending to creditworthy countries and no Bank lending to established national oil companies. From the Bank's perspective this proposal discounted its technical contribution to the design and physical aspects of an investment or exploration program and the value of its policy advice.

The inevitable conclusion, if the U.S. position prevailed, was that the Bank would then not lend at all "since we ourselves would not advance a case that we would be financing a hydrocarbon project simply to transfer resources."[140] Neither Bank management nor other member countries disagreed with the principle that the Bank's function should be residual and its lending not replace other financing available on reasonable terms; but there was considerable disagreement on the proposed U.S. guidelines. As a compromise, new energy policy guidelines were formulated that provided clearer limits on Bank lending for oil and gas exploration and development but allowed loans to national oil companies, emphasized policy leverage, and held Bank financing to a minimum necessary to achieve policy impact.

What then, is the conclusion to be drawn about U.S. influence on specific loan decisions? The record confirms that with both management and the board, U.S. views have carried great weight on loan decisions. This is not the case when the United States is required by congressional legislation to vote a specific way on designated categories of loans, because the United States acting alone can always be outvoted. But it is the case when the government has chosen to apply heavy pressure on the management and other members of the board in regard to a specific loan. Loans made despite strong opposition by the Bank's largest shareholder are the exception. However, U.S. pressure affecting the Bank's decision to make a loan to a specific country or for a specific project is also the exception. The more pervasive influence is at the level of lending policy or in the details of a loan.

ADMINISTRATION AND FINANCE. The United States has also applied strong pressure in matters of Bank administration and finance. Although instances of major disagreements between the United States and the Bank on matters of lending policy have been limited, at least before the 1980s, administrative matters have been a constant source of dispute. Four of them have been the focus of greatest attention and debate: the size of the Bank's administrative budget, increases in staff salaries and benefits, maintaining the value of Bank capital, and the evaluation and transparency of Bank activities. On all four the United States has had major influence.

The United States has not been the only member country to express strong and continuous concern about the growth of the Bank's administrative budget (most of which has occurred since the late 1970s), but it has been one of the most vocal. Concern came to a head in June 1986 when the budget proposed by management was opposed by the United States, Japan, and France, with Germany and the United Kingdom abstaining. This vote of no confidence occurred two days before Barber Conable assumed office, which led him to ask Treasury Secretary Baker, who had prevailed on him to accept the presidency, "what are you doing to me?"[141] The outcome was a major reorganization carried out in the early months of his presidency.

Conable was told by the government that there was too much fat in the system. In consultation with him McNamara agreed that reorganization was needed. But, again according to Conable, the Bank had to put together such a rich personnel separation package that he lost the support of the U.S. government for the reorganization. The Bank staff considered the reorganization disruptive and, more seriously, without clear purpose or apparent benefit to programs. Indeed, many inside and outside the Bank claimed at the time that the reorganization led to a serious mismatch between the new tasks the Bank was being pressured to take on (in environmental sensitivity, in eastern Europe and the former Soviet Union, and in private sector development) and the inadequate size and composition of the staff. Another problem, observers believed, was too little sector-specific technical expertise as a result of the reorganization. A reorganization in 1992, instigated not by the board but by Bank President Lewis T. Preston, responded to some of the concerns raised by the Conable reorganization and to the findings of an internal evaluation, commissioned by Preston in 1991, on the Bank's portfolio management.[142] That evaluation, which documented a serious deterioration in the Bank's portfolio performance, challenged the Bank's management as well as its board to institute major operational changes that incorporate but go beyond the kind of changes the United States has been demanding for many years.

The United States also criticized the high salaries of senior Bank staff as early as the 1960s. Salaries, it believed, should be compatible with U.S. civil service pay scales. But the issue did not become seriously divisive until the mid-1970s. It has since remained a point of tension, even though salary levels are now determined on the basis of a formula advanced by the United States.

In 1976 the United States successfully achieved a reduction in proposed Bank salary increases, which it regarded as excessive. This was a time when salary increases for U.S. public officials were being held down as part of a deficit-reduction, anti-inflation campaign. To win support for its position, the United States made a series of high-level representations to other member country governments. That same year, Congress linked the U.S. contribution to the Bank and the IDA to the condition that the U.S. executive director not receive compensation in excess of that paid a U.S. government official at the level of assistant secretary.

In response to the U.S. pressure, member governments agreed to form a Joint Committee on Compensation of the Bank and Fund. The committee was made up of executive directors from each institution and outside experts and was charged with recommending principles and levels of compensation. The United States further proposed that the G-5 countries commission a separate but similar study by an independent management consulting firm. Based on the recommendation of the two studies, the Bank board agreed to a compensation framework in 1979.

Underpinning the agreement was a formula proposed by the United States that would base future compensation levels and adjustments on compensation paid by "comparator organizations" in U.S. public and private sectors and similar organizations in a few selected high-income member countries (which were taken into account to ensure that the Fund and Bank would remain competitive employers in the international as well as the U.S. market). Following the adoption of its formula, the U.S. position was that the principles and mechanism were in place but questions of interpretation remained that would require watching.[143]

In subsequent years the United States made clear through high-level representations to other governments that its concerns about salary levels had not yet been resolved. In April 1986 Treasury Secretary Baker sent a letter to all governors of the Bank stating that the work of the Joint Committee on Compensation "suggests that there are serious problems in the current compensation system." The letter continues that although it is "not possible at this stage to determine precisely how much Fund and Bank salaries and benefits are out of line, or exactly what changes in the compensation system are needed," he urged governments to join the United States "in supporting a delay in any salary increase until . . . a revised compensation system has been installed."[144] In July 1989 Assistant Secretary of the Treasury Charles Dallara, in a letter to Barber Conable, strongly opposed management's recommendations on a revised system. The recommendations of the Fund and Bank management, Dallara said, were at odds in important respects with Joint Committee recommendations that the United States supported but that were "already a compromise among all participants in the Committee." Dallara concluded,

> Because the compensation issue has not been resolved satisfactorily, I fear that it could undermine our efforts to obtain funding from the Congress for both the Bank and IMF. For our part, we cannot and will not defend the new "system," which in our view does not represent a system, but rather a disparate and unwieldy collection of JCC and staff inspired elements. Both managements were fully aware of our concerns before their proposals were adopted, so I can assume you are confident of your ability to explain and defend the decisions taken and their implications.[145]

Thus after a decade and a half of contention, compensation remains a serious source of controversy. The United States is insistent on holding down excessive salaries and perks; others counter that the effect of U.S. pressure is to undermine the Bank's ability to attract high-quality staff from other countries.

The role of the dollar in the valuation of Bank capital is another matter on which the United States and the Bank (including all other members of the board) have been in dispute for many years. Although valuation is not a matter of major significance for the operations of the Bank, the U.S. refusal to abandon what is perceived as special treatment has posed financial difficulties for the Bank and antagonized other member countries. In effect, by insisting on maintaining the value of Bank capital in terms of a fixed rate of exchange between special drawing rights (SDRs) and the dollar, the United States has kept itself in the unique position among member countries of having to assume no exchange risk in its capital contributions to the Bank.

The valuation of Bank capital became an issue between the United States and the Bank when the second amendment of the Articles of Agreement of the IMF, which created the SDR, came into force. The Bank's Articles had stipulated that the standard of value for Bank capital was the U.S. dollar "of the weight and fitness in effect on July 1, 1944." This weight and fitness referred to the amount of gold for which one dollar could freely be exchanged. The Bretton Woods exchange system set the value of every other currency in terms of the dollar, which, as long as a fixed dollar price of gold prevailed, meant that every other currency also had a fixed gold value. But once the dollar was delinked from the price of gold, the executive directors of the Bank were faced with having to decide whether the successor to the 1944 gold dollar should be the SDR or the current U.S. dollar (at a rate of exchange of 1.20635, the last par value of the dollar), and whether the question should be decided through the executive directors' powers of interpretation of the Articles of Agreement or through an amendment to them. The opinion of the Bank's general counsel, and the preference of all member countries except the United States, was that the SDR should be substituted for the 1944 gold dollar on the basis of the directors' powers. The United States argued, and still argues, that a change would require an amendment because it would impose a different, flexible obligation on member governments. As a result, the United States and other countries would have to pass legislation whenever their currencies depreciated to fulfill obligations to maintain value on paid-in capital. And the United States opposed such an amendment for the same reason—that a change in SDR valuation would require legislative authorizations and appropriations for each maintenance-of-value payment the United States might be obliged to make.

For the United States the problem is more political than financial. The likely effect on the U.S. budget (positive or negative) would be minuscule. However, to accept a new maintenance-of-value obligation in the Bank would be to accept (as all other countries have had to do) an open-ended obligation to make such payments as would be required should the dollar decline against an agreed standard of value. No a priori ceiling could be set on such an obligation. Therefore, to fulfill it would require open-ended authorization and periodic appropriation legislation, which successive administrations have argued would be politically impractical even though financially trivial.

The unequal treatment that has resulted from the U.S. refusal to accept a maintenance-of-value obligation is a source of irritation among member countries. It has also posed financial headaches for the Bank from time to time. In the fall of 1987 a considerable depreciation in the U.S. dollar caused a decrease in the Bank's headroom—the difference between the amount of loans outstanding and the Bank's legal lending limit—from $18.2 billion at the end of September to $8 billion at the end of December.[146] The problem was exacerbated because negotiations for a general capital increase for the Bank had been blocked for several years by the United States. To avoid a temporary suspension of disbursements on all outstanding loans and a loss of credit standing in the markets, the Bank discussed the possibility of a special bridging operation with central banks. The aim would have been to cover further substantial dollar depreciation before Bank receipt of new subscriptions under a capital increase (not agreed to until the late 1980s). But the need for such an agreement was averted.

Over the years the United States has also persistently tried to strengthen Bank audit and evaluation procedures and has pressured the Bank to make more information on its activities available to the public.

Serious U.S. attention to audit and evaluation procedures began in Congress in the late 1960s. In June 1970 a bill authorizing the next installment of IDA funding proposed a GAO audit of the Bank. In September, Robert McNamara issued an administrative circular within the Bank, noting that since 1968 budgetary and financial controls had been strengthened by creation of the Programming and Budgeting Department, establishment of the Audit Committee of the executive directors, and strengthening the Office of Internal Auditor. In addition, the circular called for establishing an operations evaluation unit whose task would be "to review past lending operations with the central objective of establishing whether the actual benefits of the completed projects are in accordance with those expected at the time of appraisal and, in the case of divergence, the reason."[147] In mid-1971 this unit was converted into the Operations Evaluation Department. But for several years thereafter the United States urged independence from management of both the audit and evaluation operations. The OED, it argued, should be closely related to, if not directly under, the board.

In 1973 a GAO report once again recommended independent evaluations of Bank operations and activities. Legislation was proposed that would require the U.S. government to seek establishment of an independent evaluation unit in the World Bank (as Congress had previously mandated in 1967 for the International Development Bank) that would separate the postproject review system from the regular project implementation process. This step was taken by the Bank in July. The OED, along with the Internal Auditing Department, was made a separate department under a vice president who had no other direct operational responsibilities. But the matter did not end there.

In December 1973, legislation was approved requiring that the United States actively seek to establish an independent review and evaluation system under the Bank's governing body. The law also required that a statement of auditing and reporting standards be prepared by the U.S. comptroller general to assist the Bank's board in devising terms of reference for an independent review system. The comptroller general's statement, released in June 1974, proposed that the findings and related recommendations of the OED be reported to the Bank board. In response, McNamara proposed that the OED be formally linked to the board as well as to the president and that the head of the department be selected by the executive directors from a list of names put forward by the president. But the United States continued to urge even greater independence. It sought and achieved the establishment of the OED as a department that reported to the board. In addition, the staffing and design of the work program was to be the responsibility of the director general of the OED, subject to review and approval of the board on which the president, as chair, would have a significant role. After that, McNamara lost interest in the operations of the OED. And for a time it was insignificant and not a source of much internal learning. Although the United States takes credit (as in the 1982 Treasury assessment) for fostering stronger audit and evaluation procedures, one might wonder how serious it ever was about project evaluation and impact and whether the poor record on project implementation, documented in the Bank-initiated 1992 Wapenhans report, would have occurred if the United States had reached a compromise with McNamara in the mid-1970s and addressed the issue of impact consistently.[148]

Since the early 1970s the United States has also pressured the Bank to make more of its analysis available to the public. Congress first focused on the idea largely out of frustration with the Treasury's lack of Hill consultation on Bank policy issues. Although the Treasury supported Congress's efforts to institute stricter audit and evaluation procedures, it did not endorse demands for greater disclosure of Bank country papers and loan documentation, claiming that greater transparency would undermine Bank operations. Both Treasury and Bank management took the position that it was up to the borrower government to decide what documents to release. With little movement on the issue having occurred, greater transparency was again pushed aggressively in the late 1980s and early 1990s by environmental nongovernmental organizations outraged by their inability to get documentation on Bank activities deemed environmentally detrimental. The Bank is now devising a change in practice, but the new procedures are certain to remain a matter of congressional scrutiny in the early years of implementation.

Overall, U.S. influence in the Bank in matters of administration, lending, and development policy appears to have had a mix of strongly favorable and seriously detrimental effects. On the positive side, the United States has used its influence to broaden the Bank's base of donor support; it has encouraged expansion of development focus and scope of lending; and it has achieved improvements in procedures of accountability and transparency of Bank operations.

On the negative side, however, the constant U.S. pursuit of narrow objectives, driven more by short-term foreign policy aims or domestic political imperatives than by concern for the effectiveness of Bank operations, has taken an inordinate amount of the time of the Bank's high-level management and has undermined staff morale. U.S. reluctance and delay in meeting its funding commitments have obliged senior management to devote large amounts of time in replenishment negotiations and in securing bridging arrangements.

U.S. pressure has also obliged the Bank to wage a constant fight for its autonomy. As a result, its leadership and staff have "developed a 'protective shell' of beliefs and practices" that, while insulating the Bank from U.S. pressures, has hindered its effective functioning.[149] It has spent far too much time, attention, and caution in developing loan proposals and has given inadequate consideration to potential risks and alternative approaches. At the same time, the United States along with other countries has pushed the Bank, especially in recent years, into more and more areas of activity without adequate assessment of existing institutional strengths and weaknesses and without sufficient questioning of how far the institutional capabilities could be stretched. This has caused a serious deterioration in the quality of the Bank's operations. The matter of loan quality has now been starkly illuminated by the Wapenhans report, and any discussion of the sources of the problem would be incomplete without attention to the role played by the members of the board, including the United States.[150]

Furthermore, the history of the World Bank shows that the choice of its president is crucial to the life of the institution. The past three appointments have not been strong. Even McNamara's dynamic tenure could not have been anticipated—at least there was nothing to suggest that he would be a leading development figure or that he was appointed with that in mind. The United States more than any other member country can be held accountable for the leadership the Bank has enjoyed from its birth to its approaching half-century mark.

Finally, and perhaps most seriously for the future of the Bank, the combination in the 1980s of U.S. policy inconsistencies, increased assertiveness on selected issues, and dwindling support has strained relations between the United States and other member countries. There is a growing sense among them that the United States has been overplaying its hand and causing unnecessary politicization and polarization of the Bank board. This resentment has been aggravated by the increase in the 1980s of congressional micromanagement of U.S. participation in the Bank. Generally, the United States has been more successful in advancing particular issues when it has worked to build consensus than when it has been mandated by Congress to vote a particular way. One result of the growing resentment is that Japan and the major donors of Europe are focusing more on other institutions in which they exercise greater control: the European Community's development fund, the newly launched European Bank for Reconstruction and Development, and the Asian Development Bank. Yet any weakening of the World Bank would seem to run counter to the interests of the United States, which have generally been well served by Bank policies and operations and at a remarkably low cost.

A Tally of Costs and Benefits

Over the past half-century the United States has not only contributed to but has significantly benefited from the activities of the World Bank. The most comprehensive assessment to date of the costs and benefits of participation in the Bank was the 1982 Treasury report, which concluded unequivocally that the World Bank and the other multilateral development banks had been effective instruments of U.S. objectives. Referring specifically to the Bank, the report stated:

On the whole, the policies and programs of the World Bank Group have been consistent with U.S. interests. This is particularly true in terms of general country allocation questions and sensitive policy issues. The international character of the World Bank, its corporate structure, the strength of the management team, and the Bank's weighted voting structure have ensured broad consistency between its policies and practices and the long term economic and political objectives of the United States.[151]

Referring to all the multilateral development banks together, it noted that they had been "most effective in contributing to the achievement of our *global economic and financial objectives* and thereby also helping us in our long term political/strategic interests." They were less effective instruments, however, for achieving short-term policy objectives, where identification of the assistance with the United States was important and, it emphasized, there was "room for improvement in terms of encouraging more effective economic policy reform in individual [less developed countries]."[152]

One of the main ways U.S. interests have been served is by Bank lending—far beyond an amount the United States was willing to provide bilaterally—to countries of strategic or economic importance to the United States. Indeed, as has been frequently noted in executive branch testimony before Congress in defense of World Bank funding requests and reiterated in the Treasury assessment, most Bank lending has gone to those countries. The point is made, for example, in a letter from President Reagan to Robert Michel, the Republican leader in the House, urging support for the 1988 general capital increase: "The Bank commits the vast majority of its funds in support of specific investment projects in the middle income developing nations. These are mostly nations (such as the Philippines, Egypt, Pakistan, Turkey, Morocco, Tunisia, Mexico, Argentina, Indonesia and Brazil) that are strategically and economically important to the United States."[153]

Bank lending has also served broad U.S. economic interests in the building of a free, open and stable international economic system. According to the Treasury assessment, "by promoting economic and social development in the Third World, fostering market-oriented economic policies, and preserving a reputation for impartiality and competence, the MDBs encourage developing countries to participate more fully in an international system based on liberalized trade and capital flows. . . . This means expanding opportunities for U.S. exports, investment, and finance." In addition, the ability of the multilateral banks

Table 4. World Bank and International Development Association Operations and U.S. Balance of Payments, Cumulative, 1946–91
Millions of constant 1990 dollars

Operations	Total
World Bank	
Current account	
Procurement of goods[a]	26,060.7
Interest to bond holders[b]	20,169.7
Interest to loan holders	626.5
Administrative expenses including issuance cost of bonds[c]	10,948.7
Currency swap activity	−4,357.4
Investment income	16,916.7
Balance on current account	36,531.4
Capital account	
Assets	
U.S. payment of 1 percent subscription	66.4
U.S. payment of 9 percent subscription	597.3
U.S. payments[d]	126.0
Local currency releases[e]	1,071.2
Net bond sales[f]	13,623.4
Net loan sales	−696.9
Total assets	14,787.4
Liabilities	
Investments with maturities over one year	20,645.3
Investments with maturities of one year or less	−110.2
Total liabilities	20,535.1
Balance of capital account	5,747.7
Net change	42,279.1

to design and implement high-quality development loans has contributed to a more efficient process of development assistance. Their "capability to administer programs productively and efficiently ensures cost effectiveness and can maximize the use of scarce development resources."[154]

The United States has achieved these benefits for a remarkably low financial expenditure. Two points are relevant here. First, U.S. investment in the Bank and its contributions to IDA have been highly leveraged. In the case of the Bank the United States had paid in $1,857,100,000 of the $218,209,900,000 provided in loans as of mid-1992. In the case of IDA it has contributed a relatively larger share of the funds over the years, and the leveraging effect has been less but by no means insignificant. As of mid-1992 it had contributed $18,081,500,000 of the total $71,065,000,000 lent.[155]

Table 4. (Continued)

Operations	Total
IDA	
Current account	
Procurement of goods[g]	5,112.3
Administrative expenses	4,612.6
Investment income[h]	−642.2
Balance on current account	9,082.8
Capital account	
Assets	
Subscriptions and contributions[i]	18,634.4
Total assets	18,634.4
Liabilities	
Investments with maturities over one year	104.9
Investments with maturities of one year or less	−117.8
Total liabilities	−12.9
Balance of capital account	−18,647.3
Net change	−9,564.6

Source: World Bank Treasury Department.

a. Includes procurements specifically identified as originating in the United States and the same proportion of procurement not identifiable by country of origin.

b. Interest payments to U.S. bond holders living in the United States.

c. Administrative expenses incurred in U.S. dollars in the United States, including the issuance cost of bonds.

d. Capital subscription paid by the United States.

e. Capital subscription in 18 percent national currencies released in U.S. dollars and used for loan disbursements.

f. Bonds sold for delayed delivery are included in the year in which settlement is made.

g. Includes procurements specifically identified as originating in the United States and the same proportion of procurement not identifiable by country of origin.

h. For years from inception through June 30, 1964, the ratio of average of U.S. investments to average total investments was applied to total investment income. For fiscal 1965 and subsequent years, the amount shown is the actual amount as computed for the statement "Statistical Summary of Funds Received by Source."

i. Excludes notes not encashed.

Second, the net effect of the World Bank Group on the U.S. balance of payments has been positive (table 4). One reason is that the United States has received substantial procurement benefits: World Bank procurements have totaled $26,060,700,000. In addition, interest payments to U.S. bondholders living in the United States have been $20,169,700,000 and administrative expenses incurred in U.S. dollars in the United States, $10,948,700,000. These amounts have been the major factors contributing to a total net balance of payments effect (in real terms) of $42,279,000,000, which more than compensates for the net negative effect of support for IDA of some $9,564,500,000. Obviously, U.S. contributions to the Bank entail an opportunity cost, but taking into account the political and economic interests served, the conclusion about U.S.-World Bank relations is one of shared benefit.

Conclusion

A number of broad observations can be drawn from this review of the history of the U.S. relations with the World Bank from 1945 to the early 1990s.

More than any other country, the United States has shaped and directed the institutional evolution, policies, and activities of the World Bank. And for the most part, U.S. participation has supported the institution's rise to prominence in development cooperation. The United States has applied pressure both to stop and to encourage particular loan agreements, but the greater influence has been at the level of policy and institutional evolution and growth. Much, though not all, of what the United States has promoted has helped foster constructive changes in the Bank, including the increase in agriculture and poverty-oriented lending, the increasing concentration of IDA lending on the poorest countries, the introduction, after some reluctance, of structural adjustment lending, and the recent attention to environmental sustainability and transparency of transactions.

Although U.S. support for the World Bank has shown some ups and downs, it has been more stable than other elements of U.S. economic assistance. This stability has largely been due to the value to the United States of the leveraging effect of contributions to the Bank, perceptions of the Bank's relative effectiveness as a provider of both development financing and policy advice, and the view held by most administrations and members of Congress that the Bank contributes to the broad interest of the United States in a growing and open world economy. With the exception of Reagan's first administration, all administrations since the Bank's founding have advanced these views and, with only few exceptions, leading Republicans and Democrats in Congress have concurred.

Criticisms of the World Bank from various voices in the United States have, however, greatly intensified since the mid-1970s. These opinions have come from all points on the political spectrum, including churches and other NGOs, the traditional bulwarks of support for development assistance. In part the criticism reflects the increased prominence of the Bank in development and the closer scrutiny it receives. In part it reflects changing ideas about development, not all of which suit Bank lending operations as easily as the earlier preoccupations with infrastructure development. And in part the criticism reflects the loss of a clear sense of purpose and direction in U.S. development policy, for which the Bank is but one instrument.

U.S. policy toward the World Bank has always reflected an underlying ambivalence toward both development assistance and multilateral cooperation. Recognizing the long-term benefits of the relatively efficient and relatively depoliticized development financing the Bank offers, the United States has also looked upon it as an instrument of foreign policy that was expected to be responsive to short-term U.S. positions. As a result, U.S. policy toward the Bank and the positions it has taken within the Bank have been erratic, often reflecting more the ebb and flow of U.S. politics and foreign policy than a coherent view of the Bank's development financing and a steadfast concern for the effectiveness of its operations.

Two features of the policy process have strongly influenced the character of U.S. World Bank policy. On the one hand the dominant role of the Treasury has limited the development content of U.S. policy and participation in the Bank. On the other hand Congress and, indirectly, NGOs have been instrumental in designing U.S. Bank policy. This involvement has influenced Treasury's dominant role, keeping development concerns in sharper focus in the formation of U.S. policy than might otherwise have been the case. But Congress has also been a conduit for particularistic views on Bank lending and has been responsible for the proliferation of restrictions and demands on the Bank that have been unilaterally promoted by the United States. Debates in Congress have also led to frequent failures on the part of the United States to deliver its share of negotiated replenishments within an internationally agreed time frame and have forced other countries to make up for temporary U.S. shortfalls to avoid a break in IDA lending. Both kinds of actions have eroded U.S. influence on the board of the Bank and on the Bank's efficiency.

Finally, the United States has also pressed successfully for ever greater burden sharing by other developed country members of the Bank. But it has resisted the power sharing that ought to go along with their growing financial contributions. If the United States wants to see the Bank continue to function and evolve in ways consistent with U.S. interests, it will have to dedicate effective personnel to its Bank policy positions (including the position of U.S. executive director), arrive at an understanding with Congress on the major priorities of U.S. policy toward the Bank, structure development policy expertise into its Bank policymaking process, and engage actively with other member countries in consensus building. It must shed the ideological strictures of the past decade of U.S. Bank policy and develop with other countries, notably Japan, the policy guidance for and oversight of the challenging new era of the World Bank's second half-century.

Notes

1. The U.S. role was acknowledged by John Maynard Keynes in his opening remarks at the Bretton Woods Conference when he observed that the international bank draft document being considered was due "primarily to the initiative and ability of the United States Treasury." Edward S. Mason and Robert E. Asher, *The World Bank since Bretton Woods* (Brookings, 1973), p. 13.

2. This section on the founding of the Bank draws heavily on several histories, including Mason and Asher, *World Bank since Bretton Woods*; Richard N. Gardner, *Sterling-Dollar Diplomacy in Current Perspective* (Columbia University Press, 1980); and Robert W. Oliver, *Early Plans for a World Bank*, Princeton Studies in International Finance no. 29, Princeton University, 1971.

3. Harry Dexter White, quoted in Mason and Asher, *World Bank since Bretton Woods*, p. 18. The same point was stressed by American economist Alvin H. Hansen, who proposed in 1944 an international development and investment bank. According to Hansen, in the absence of basic developmental projects financed by public funds, private investments in many cases could not be undertaken. See "World Institutions for Stability and Expansion," Foreign Affairs, vol. 22 (January 1944), pp. 248–55.

4. Consideration was also given to establishing an international development corporation and commodity price stabilization mechanism, but these elements as well as a larger capital base for the Bank were rejected in discussions within the U.S. government before the plan for the Bank was presented to other countries.

5. Quoted in Mason and Asher, *World Bank since Bretton Woods*, p. 12.

6. C. Fred Bergsten, working paper of the Study Group on International Financial Institutions, Council on Foreign Relations, New York, 1980, p. 4. Cited with permission of the author.

7. Gardner, *Sterling-Dollar Diplomacy*, pp. 258–59.

8 . Quoted in ibid., p. 258.

9 . Quoted in ibid., p. 76.

10. Davidson Sommers, Address to Professional Staff Meeting on "The Early Days of the Bank," Washington, May 5, 1960, pp. 5, 7.

11. Kai Bird, The Chairman: John J. McCloy, *The Making of the American Establishment* (Simon and Schuster, 1992), p. 283.

12. Ibid., p. 285. Their enthusiasm may have been heightened by the fact that the Republicans won a resounding victory in the November 1946 elections.

13. Sommers, "Early Days of the Bank," p. 10.

14. Bird, *Chairman*, p. 286.

15. Jonathan E. Sanford, *U.S. Foreign Policy and Multilateral Development Banks* (Boulder, Colo.: Westview Press, 1982), p. 44.

16. Ibid., p. 43.

17. Mason and Asher, *World Bank since Bretton Woods*, p. 34.

18. Sanford, *U.S. Foreign Policy*, p. 43.

19. Gardner, *Sterling-Dollar Diplomacy*, p. 142.

20. The phrase "a dollar bank" and this summary are drawn largely from Mason and Asher, *World Bank since Bretton Woods*, pp. 105–49.

21. Ibid., p. 779.

22. Ibid., pp. 43–44.

23. To gain investors' support, Bank president John McCloy, his chosen vice president, Robert L. Garner, a fellow U.S. banker and businessman, and U.S. executive director Eugene Black spent much of the spring of 1947 on the road, giving speeches at bankers' conventions and lobbying various state legislatures.

24. This point is drawn from quotations from several World Bank oral histories cited in Mason and Asher, *World Bank since Bretton Woods*.

25. Bird, *Chairman*, pp. 292–93.

26. James H. Weaver, *The International Development Association* (Praeger, 1965), p. 31.

27. Bronislaw E. Matecki, *Establishment of the International Finance Corporation and United States Policy* (Praeger, 1957), p. 149.

28. Ibid.

29. Quoted in Sanford, *U.S. Foreign Policy*, p. 46.

30. Congress formally authorized U.S. membership in the IFC in August 1955 and approved an initial U.S. capital subscription of $35 million out of a total capital base of $100 million.

31. Quoted in Sanford, *U.S. Foreign Policy*, p. 47.

32. For a discussion of the evolution of these views see, for example, Congressional Research Service, "Soviet Policy and United States Response in the Third World," March 1981, p. 5.

33. Robert J. Berg and David F. Gordon, eds., *Cooperation for International Development: The United States and the Third World in the 1990s* (London: Lynne Rienner, 1989), pp. 1–2.

34. Mason and Asher, *World Bank since Bretton Woods*, p. 411.

35. According to Robert W. Oliver in his forthcoming biography of George Woods, "everyone remembered Eugene Black as a warm person who entertained Congressmen, but George Woods entertained little." *The Anguish of George Woods*, chap. 8, p. 29.

36. Paul A. Volcker and Toyoo Gyohten, *Changing Fortunes: The World's Money and the Threat to American Leadership* (Times Books, 1992), chap. 2.

37. Bank Vice President Burke Knapp suggested at the time that it would also be useful to have the Department of State designate the U.S. alternate executive director as a way to keep the department informed of Bank policies and operations. But after the removal of Emilio Collado as the first director, the

Treasury Department had gained increasing control of the U.S. multilateral development bank policy process, usually collaborating but at times disagreeing with the State Department on the handling of individual country cases as well as broad policy toward the Bank.

38. Angus Maddison, *The World Economy in the 20th Century* (Paris: OECD, 1989), p. 113.

39. Deputy Treasury Secretary Charles E. Walker, quoted in National Advisory Council on International Monetary and Financial Policies, *Annual Report* (Washington, 1972), p. 12.

40. Robert E. Asher, *Development Assistance in the Seventies: Alternatives for the United States* (Brookings, 1970), p. 19.

41. Congressional Research Service, "Soviet Policy and United States Response," p. 1.

42. For a detailed discussion of Congress's role in U.S. World Bank policymaking, see Jonathan E. Sanford, "U.S. Policy toward the Multilateral Development Banks: The Role of Congress," *George Washington Journal of International Law and Economics*, vol. 22 (1988), pp. 1–115.

43. For a discussion of this problem see Lars Schoultz, "Politics, Economics, and U.S. Participation in Multilateral Development Banks," *International Organization*, vol. 36 (summer 1982), pp. 537–74.

44. See, for example, Rudolph A. Petersen, "U.S. Foreign Assistance in the 1970s: A New Approach," Task Force on International Development, Washington, 1970; Dexter Perkins, "Development Assistance in the New Administration: Report of the President's General Advisory Committee on Foreign Assistance Programs," Agency for International Development, Washington, 1968; and Lester Pearson, *Partners in Development: Report of the Commission on International Development* (Praeger, 1969).

45. Asher, Development Assistance in the Seventies, esp. pp. 119–24.

46. Richard M. Nixon, message to Congress, October 15, 1970. Quoted in Sanford, *U.S. Foreign Policy*, p. 58.

47. William Clark, "Robert McNamara at the World Bank," *Foreign Affairs*, vol. 60 (Fall 1981), p. 176.

48. See, for example, Stephen S. Rosenfeld, "Robert S. McNamara and the Wiser Use of Power," *World Opinion*, July 3, 1973, pp. 19–20.

49. Clark, "Robert McNamara," p. 176.

50. Ibid., p. 178. This 1974 attempt had a parallel in 1980–82 following the second oil shock when the incoming Reagan administration rejected an initiative to create an energy affiliate, as discussed later.

51. Kissinger was concerned that, following OPEC's actions, other third world countries would try to form cartels in strategic commodities. Therefore one of his initiatives was for a resource development bank. McNamara, as indicated in minutes of the meetings of his president's council, took Kissinger's proposal as a signal that the United States would support Bank lending in the mining and production of minerals, but this was not to prove so.

52. Statement by William E. Simon, *Summary Proceedings of the 1976 Annual*

Meetings of the Boards of Governors (Manila: IBRD, 1976), p. 190.

53. Charles A. Cooper, working paper for the Study Group on International Financial Institutions, Council on Foreign Relations, New York, March 1980. Cited with permission of the author. See also National Advisory Council on International Monetary and Financial Policy, *Annual Report to the President and to the Congress, July 1, 1975–June 30, 1976* (Washington, 1977).

54. John Lewis and Richard Webb interview with Robert S. McNamara, May 10, 1991, transcript, p. 7.

55. Sanford, U.S. *Foreign Policy*, p. 120.

56. *Foreign Assistance Act of 1973*, P.L. 93-189.

57. Bergsten, working paper, p. 14.

58. The amendment, adding section 21 to the 1959 Inter-American Development Bank Act, section 11 to the 1960 *International Development Association Act*, and section 18 to the 1966 *Asian Development Bank Act*.

59. Sanford, *U.S. Foreign Policy*; and Jessica Pernitz Einhorn, *Expropriation Politics* (Lexington, Mass: Lexington Books, 1974).

60. House Committee on Appropriations, *Foreign Assistance and Related Programs Appropriation Bill, 1972*, report 92-711, 92 Cong. 1 sess. (1971), p. 33.

61. See, for example, General Accounting Office, "More Effective United States Participation Needed in World Bank and International Development Association," 1973; and General Accounting Office, "Effectiveness of the World Bank's Independent Review and Evaluation System," 1978.

62. Senate Committee on Appropriations, *Foreign Assistance and Related Programs Appropriation Bill, 1978*, report 95-352, 95 Cong. 1 sess. (July 1977), p. 124.

63. House Committee on Appropriations, *Foreign Assistance and Related Programs Appropriation Bill, 1978*, report 95-417, 95 Cong. 1 sess. (June 1977), pp. 72–73.

64. Although the executive branch countered most of the charges, the report was picked up in the press and darkened the Bank's image with both Congress and the public at large.

65. Senate Committee on Appropriations, *Foreign Assistance and Related Programs Appropriation Bill, 1975*, report 94-39, 94 Cong. 1 sess. (March 1975), p. 142.

66. U.S. civil service salary scales were lower than those of some other developed countries and salaries were capped for much of the time after 1968, which added to resentment of rising salaries in an international institution just blocks away from the Treasury Department and other offices.

67. Senate Committee on Appropriations, *Foreign Operations, Export Financing, and Related Programs Appropriation Bill, 1990*, report 101-131, 101 Cong. 1 sess. (September 1989), p. 72.

68. For a review of the congressional debate and legislation, see House Committee on Foreign Affairs, *Congress and Foreign Policy, 1977* (1978).

69. For review of the Congressional debate and legislation see House Committee on Foreign Affairs, *Congress and Foreign Policy, 1978* (1979), esp.

pp. 88–92.

70. Testimony of W. Michael Blumenthal, *Nomination of W. Michael Blumenthal*, Hearings before the Senate Committee on Finance, 95 Cong. 1 sess. (GPO, 1977), quoted in Sanford, *U.S. Foreign Policy*, p. 68.

71. Mark F. McGuire and Vernon W. Ruttan, "Lost Directions: U.S. Foreign Assistance Policy since New Directions," *Journal of Developing Areas*, vol. 24 (January 1990), p. 137.

72. For example, McNamara was invited to participate in National Security Council meetings in the White House that dealt with gaining support for IDA 5 and the general capital increase that the Ford administration had opposed.

73. Letter from Jimmy Carter to Clarence D. Long, chairman of the Subcommittee on Foreign Operations and Related Agencies, House Committee on Appropriations, October 6, 1977. *Congressional Record*, vol. 123 (October 18, 1977), p. 34093.

74. Schoultz, "Politics, Economics, and U.S. Participation," pp. 568–69.

75. Letter from Robert S. McNamara to Clarence Long, chairman of the Subcommittee on Foreign Operations and Related Agencies, House Committee on Appropriations, November 1, 1979. Reproduced in *Congressional Record* (December 3, 1979), p. 34415. Reference to a second letter from McNamara apologizing to Treasury Secretary G. William Miller for not going through usual channels is in Bartram S. Brown, *The United States and the Politicization of the World Bank* (London: Kegan Paul, 1992), p. 189. No subsequent loans have been made to Vietnam.

76. Discussion of the politicization of MDB legislative action draws heavily on Catherine Gwin, interview with Jonathan Sanford, Congressional Research Service, May 14, 1991.

77. See, for example, the remarks of Congressman David Obey stating that he had been so attacked, in *Foreign Assistance and Related Programs Appropriations for 1982*, pt. 4, Hearings before the House Committee on Appropriations, 97 Cong. 1 sess. (GPO, 1981), pp. 186–88.

78. House Committee on Foreign Affairs, *Congress and Foreign Policy*, 1981 (GPO, 1982), p. 50. A letter from President Reagan did not, however, end the Republican party's attack on Democratic supporters of the World Bank and IMF up for reelection. In 1983 Phil Gramm proposed that the U.S. executive director to the IMF be directed to oppose any use of IMF credit to "communist dictatorships." His motion passed in the House 242–185, and two weeks later the National Republican Congressional Committee began distributing press releases in the districts of 21 Democrats who voted against the Gramm amendment, charging them with voting in favor of communism. The Republican administration having sought the quota increase, House Democrats demanded and received a letter from President Reagan expressing his strong appreciation for their support of the IMF legislation and their opposition to the amendment. See Juan Williams and Hobart Rowen, "Reagan Thanks Democrats for IMF Bill Votes," *Washington Post*, October 25, 1983, p. A4.

79. The Carter administration also initiated monetary and fiscal actions

(continued by the Reagan administration) aimed at bringing down double-digit inflation that had a far more devastating immediate effect on developing economies than aid transfers helped them. For a discussion of these effects, see John P. Lewis, "Can We Escape the Path of Mutual Injury?" in John P. Lewis and Valeriana Kallab, eds., *U.S. Foreign Policy and the Third World Agenda, 1983* (Praeger for Overseas Development Council, 1983), pp. 7–48.

80. "1980 Republican Platform Text," *Congressional Quarterly Almanac*, vol. 36 (Washington: Congressional Quarterly, 1980), pp. 58-B, 83-B.

81. David A. Stockman, *The Triumph of Politics: How the Reagan Revolution Failed* (Harper and Row, 1986), pp. 116–19.

82. Although other donors objected to this unilateral move, they adhered to the rds over and above their regular three-year schedule and later agreed to provide additional funds to enable IDA to continue its regular operations during the fourth year.

83. Department of the Treasury, *United States Participation in the Multilateral Development Banks in the 1980s* (1982).

84. Opening remarks by President Ronald Reagan, *Summary Proceedings of 1983 Annual Meetings of the Boards of Governors* (Washington: IBRD, 1983), p. 2.

85. Quoted in Hobart Rowen, "U.S. May End Support of IDA Programs," *Washington Post*, February 5, 1985, p. C1.

86. For early indications of impending problems, see *Multinational Corporations and Foreign Policy*, pt. 15, Hearings before the Subcommittee on Multinational Corporations of the Senate Committee of Foreign Relations, 94 Cong. 1 sess. (GPO, July–October 1975); and *The Wittaveen Facility and the OPEC Financial Surpluses*, Hearings before the Senate Subcommittee on Foreign Economic Policy, 95 Cong. 1 sess. (GPO, September–October 1977). For a review of the unfolding of the international debt crisis see Karin Lissakers, *Banks, Borrowers, and the Establishment* (Basic Books, 1991).

87. Joseph Kraft, *The Mexican Rescue* (New York: Group of Thirty, 1984), p. 11.

88. William R. Cline, "The Baker Plan and Brady Reformulation: An Evaluation," in Richard O'Brien and Ingred Iversen, eds., *Finance and International Economics*, vol. 3 (Oxford University Press for American Express Bank Review, 1989).

89. See, for example, Rudiger Dornbusch, ed., *Alternative Solutions to Developing-Country Debt Problems* (Washington: American Enterprise Institute, 1989).

90. Debate on debt-related issues held up approval on the U.S. contribution to the Bank's general capital increase for over a year in 1988–89. See Richard Lawrence, "World Bank Contribution Hinges on Congressional Compromise," *Journal of Commerce*, August 12, 1988, pp. 1A, 10A; and Hobart Rowen, "David Obey's World Bank Crusade," *Washington Post*, November 12, 1989, pp. H1, H4.

91. See, for example, Third World Debt Panel of the Economic Policy Council of the United Nations Association of the United States of America, "Third World

Debt: A Reexamination of Long-Term Management" (New York, September 7, 1988).

92. Anne O. Krueger, *Economic Policies at Cross-Purposes* (Brookings, 1993), p. 97.

93. Letter from Ernest Stern, World Bank senior vice president for finance, to Charles Dallara, assistant secretary of the Treasury for Policy Development, March 7, 1989.

94. Catherine Gwin, interview with Paul Volcker, May 27, 1992.

95. World Bank internal memorandum, May 2, 1990.

96. World Bank internal memorandum, March 29, 1990 (confidential).

97. Krueger, *Economic Policies at Cross-Purposes*, chap. 5.

98. The veto applies to matters requiring more than a simple majority, notably decisions regarding the Articles, not specific loans. Japan's willingness to provide more of the IDA 8 replenishment had been made contingent on substantial expansion of its Bank share, which would make its share significantly greater than that of Germany and signal that it stood second only to the United States. A major improvement in Japan's position could only occur, however, if the United States agreed to let its own share slip below 20 percent (which was the percentage that ensured its veto). During the IDA 8 negotiations the United States indicated its intention to seek a change in the Articles to enable it to retain its veto with only 15 percent of total share and thereby accommodate an increase for Japan without sacrificing its own position.

99. The discussion of environmental policy issues from early 1983 through mid-1987 draws heavily on Bruce Rich, "Greens Lay Siege to the Crystal Palace," a chapter in a forthcoming book on the World Bank and the environmental movement.

100. Ibid., msp. 98.

101. *Department of Defense Appropriations Act, 1986* (H.J. Res. 465).

102. *International Development and Finance Act of 1989* (H.R. 2494).

103. Catherine Gwin, interview with Eugene Rotberg, Washington, D.C. , August 14, 1991.

104. Bank memorandum, April 6, 1984.

105. Catherine Gwin, interview with Eugene Rotberg.

106. John Lewis and Richard Webb, interview with Barber Conable, Washington, D.C., May 8, 1991.

107. For the 1951 figure see Mason and Asher, *World Bank since Bretton Woods*, table 4-3; for the 1991 figure see *World Bank, Human Resources Data, Annual Review, FY 1993* (Washington, 1993), p. B-1.

108. See Sanford, *U.S. Foreign Policy*. See also statement by C. Fred Bergsten, *Hearings before the Subcommittee on International Development Institutions and Finance of the Committee on Banking, Finance and Urban Affairs*, 96 Cong. 1 sess. (GPO, April 24, 1979); and statement, *Hearings before the Subcommittee on Foreign Operations of the Committee on Appropriations*, 96 Cong. 1 sess. (GPO, March 27, 1979).

109. This included for a time the U.S. executive director, but as interest in the

Bank waned so too did the quality of the appointees. After the first few appointments, the executive director has been selected by the Treasury and has been on its staff. The most notable decline in quality and stature came not surprisingly in the first half of the 1980s when the Treasury itself was openly critical of the Bank.

110. Former Treasury official C. Fred Bergsten in testimony before a subcommittee of the House in April 1979 made this point, although, for domestic political reasons, he overstated the strength of U.S. influence. According to Bergsten, starting in 1972 the World Bank began to alter the nature of its lending to reach the poorest populations in borrowing countries more directly. "The U.S. Government strongly influenced this change in direction, and the Congress played a major part in so doing. The United States was able to attract wide support within the Bank and among member countries for the reaching-the-poor thrust, and the progress made is unarguable." Statement, *Hearings before the Subcommittee on Foreign Operations of the Committee on Appropriations*, 96 Cong. 1 sess. (GPO, April 3, 1979).

111. Walter S. Mossberg, "World Bank's Conable Runs into Criticism on Poor Nations' Debt," Wall Street Journal, June 21, 1988, pp. 1, 25.

112. J. Burke Knapp, "Determination of Priorities and the Allocation of Resources," in John P. Lewis and Ishan Kapur, eds., *The World Bank Group, Multilateral Aid and the 1970s* (Lexington, Mass.: Lexington Books, 1973), p. 50.

113. Bird, *Chairman*, p. 291.

114. "World Bank Loan to Poland Stymied," *New York Times*, November 5, 1947, p. 43. See also Robert W. Oliver, *International Economic Co-operation and the World Bank* (MacMillan, 1975), pp. 241, 244–45.

115. Bird, Chairman, p. 295–96.

116. International Bank for Reconstruction and Development, Second Annual Report, (Washington, 1947), p. 17, quoted in Brown, *United States and Politicization*, pp. 128–29.

117. This summary account draws on Mason and Asher, *World Bank since Bretton Woods*, pp. 627–42.

118. Ibid., p. 638.

119. International Bank for Reconstruction and Development, *Policies and Operations* (Washington, 1969), cited in Brown, *United States and Politicization*, pp. 162–63.

120. In its statement before the 1972 World Bank's annual meeting, the Chilean government protested that its rationalization policy was the reason for the country's having received no new loans during the twenty-two months of the Allende administration, despite having submitted elaborate project proposals. International Bank for Reconstruction and Development, *Summary Proceedings of the 1972 Annual Meetings of the Boards of Governors* (Washington, 1972), p. 55.

121. Confidential memorandum from Mahbub ul Haq to Robert McNamara, April 1976.

122. Jonathan Sanford, "The MDBs and the Suspension of Lending to Allende's Chile," Congressional Research Service, December 13, 1974, supports

McNamara's claim.

123. World Bank," Chile and the World Bank," white paper, cited in Brown, *United States and Politicization*, p. 167.

124. "A Private Note on Internal Bank Deliberations on Vietnam," September 21, 1979; and confidential memorandum from Shahid Husain to Robert McNamara, August 31, 1979.

125. Husain, memorandum, August 31, 1979; and Susan Drake, "Vietnam's Troubles," *Newsweek*, August 20, 1979.

126. Internal memorandum, December 21, 1984 (confidential).

127. Cable from Joaquin Cuadra Chamorro, Nicaraguan minister of finance, to David Knox, December 19, 1984.

128. "The Ironies That Built Japan, Inc.," *Washington Post*, July 18, 1993, p. H12.

129. Jacques J. Polak, "The World Bank and the International Monetary Fund," in Richard Webb and Davesh Kapur, eds., *History of the World Bank* (Brookings, forthcoming).

130. This sequence of events was confirmed in interviews, including Catherine Gwin, interview with Charles Dallara, New York, October 2, 1991, and is corroborated in Polak, op.cit.

131. Ibid.

132. Paul Mosley, Jane Harrigan, and John Toye, *Aid and Power: The World Bank and Policy-based Lending*, vol. 1 (London: Routledge, 1991), p. 128.

133. Catherine Gwin, interview with Burke Knapp, Washington, D.C., September 25, 1992.

134. Internal Bank documents from the period show that Barber Conable rejected the recommendations of Ernest Stern that the Bank provide loans to assist steel sector restructuring in cases other than China and Mexico. Conable was presumably influenced by his knowledge of the strength of opposition on this issue in Congress and the administration.

135. Jonathan Friedland, "Inside Job at the World Bank," *South*, no. 83 (September 1987), pp. 9–10.

136. Catherine Gwin, interview with Edward Fried, Washington, D.C., July 16, 1992.

137. Clyde H. Farnsworth, "U.S. Rejects Proposal to Form World Bank Energy Affiliate," *New York Times*, August 13, 1981, "Sunday Week in Review," p. 15.

138. World Bank internal memorandum, April 6, 1984.

139. Ibid.; and World Bank internal memorandum, May 9, 1984.

140. World Bank internal memorandum, April 6, 1984.

141. John Lewis and Richard Webb, interview with Barber Conable, Washington, D.C., May 8, 1991.

142. Portfolio Management Task Force, *Effective Implementation: Key to Development Impact* (Washington: World Bank, 1992).

143. See National Advisory Council on International Monetary and Financial Policies, *Annual Report, Fiscal Year 1981* (Washington, 1981), pp. 41–42.

144. Letter from Secretary of the Treasury James A. Baker to each of the governors of the Bank, April 25, 1986.

145. Letter from Assistant Secretary of the Treasury Charles H. Dallara to Barber Conable, July 10, 1989.

146. At that time, each 1 percent depreciation of the dollar vis-à-vis other G-7 currencies eroded the Bank's headroom by $800 million.

147. Robert S. McNamara, administrative circular, September 2, 1970, p. 1.

148. Portfolio Management Task Force, "Effective Implementation: Key to Development Impact," World Bank, September 1992.

149. William Ascher, "The World Bank and U.S. Control," in Margaret Karns and Karen Mingst, eds., *The United States and Multilateral Institutions* (Boston: Unwin Human, 1990), p. 116.

150. Portfolio Management Task Force, "Effective Implementation."

151. Department of the Treasury, *United States Participation in Multilateral Development Banks*, p. 59.

152. Ibid., p. 4.

153. Letter from President Ronald Reagan to Representative Robert Michel, June 10, 1988, p. 1.

154. Department of the Treasury, *United States Participation in Multilateral Development Banks*, pp. 48, 52.

155. World Bank data.